THE
HARBINGER

THE

HARBINGER

JONATHAN CAHN

THE HARBINGER by Jonathan Cahn
Published by FrontLine
Charisma Media/Charisma House Book Group
600 Rinehart Road
Lake Mary, Florida 32746

Unless otherwise noted, all Scripture quotations are from the New King James Version of the Bible. Copyright © 1979, 1980, 1982 by Thomas Nelson, Inc., publishers. Used by permission.

Cover design by Justin Evans
Design Director: Bill Johnson

Visit the author's website at www.hopeoftheworld.org.

ISBN 978-1-62090-096-3

While the author has made every effort to provide accurate Internet addresses at the time of publication, neither the publisher nor the author assumes any responsibility for errors or for changes that occur after publication.

This publication has been translated in Spanish under the title *El presagio*, copyright © 2012 by Jonathan Cahn, published by Casa Creación, a Charisma Media company. All rights reserved.
Printed in the United States of America

What you are about to read is presented in the form of a story, but what is contained within the story is real.

Contents

אָ ה

Chapter 1

An Ancient Mystery

א ה

"AN ANCIENT MYSTERY that holds the secret of America's future."

"Yes."

"What would I think?"

"Yes, what would you think?"

"I'd think it was a plot for a movie. Is that it? Is that what you're presenting…a movie manuscript?"

"No."

"A plot for a novel?"

"No."

"Then what?"

He was silent.

"Then what?" she repeated.

He paused to carefully consider what he was about to say and how to say it. Her reputation among those in media was that of a woman who neither wasted her time nor indulged those who did. She was not known to suffer fools gladly. The discussion could meet an abrupt end at any given moment and there would be no second chance with her. The fact that there had even been a meeting in the first place, that she had even agreed to it, and that he was now sitting in her office, high above the streets of Manhattan, was nothing short of a miracle—and he knew it. He had only one concern—the message. It didn't even occur to him to remove his black leather overcoat, nor had anyone offered to remove it for him. Leaning forward in his chair, he gave her his answer, slowly, cautiously, carefully deliberating every word.

"An ancient mystery…that holds the secret of America's

future...and on which its future hangs. And it's *not fiction*—it's real."

She was quiet. At first, he took the silence as a positive sign, an indication that he was getting through. But then she spoke and quickly dispelled the notion.

"An Indiana Jones movie," she said. "An ancient mystery hidden for thousands of years under the sands of the Middle East...but now revealed...and upon it hangs the fate of the entire world!"

Her flippancy provoked him to become all the more resolute. "But it's not fiction," he repeated. "It's real."

"What would I say?" she asked.

"Yes, what would you say?"

"I'd say you were crazy."

"Perhaps I am," he said with a slight smile. "Nevertheless...it's real."

"If you're not crazy, then you're joking...or you're doing this all for dramatic effect...part of a presentation. But you can't be serious."

"But I *am serious*."

She paused for a moment, staring into the eyes of her guest, attempting to ascertain whether he was sincere or not.

"So you are," she said.

"So I am," he replied, "and you have no idea how much so."

It was then that her expression changed. Up to that point it had suggested a trace of amused interest. It now turned to that of total disengagement.

"No, I guess I don't. Listen, I believe you're a sincere man, but...I'm really...I'm really very busy, and I don't have time for..."

"Mrs. Goren."

"That's Go*ren*. The accent's on the last syllable. But *Ana* is fine."

"Ana, you have nothing to lose by listening. Just go on the slight possibility..."

"That you're not crazy?"

"That too," he said. "But the slight possibility that what I'm saying could actually be true, even the slight possibility that there could be something in what I'm telling you, even for that slightest of possibilities…for just that…it would be important enough to warrant your time. You need to hear me out."

She sat back in her chair and stared at him, making no attempt to hide her skepticism.

"You still think I'm crazy."

"Fully," she said.

"For argument's sake, let's say you're right. I *am* crazy. Indulge me, as a public service."

She smiled.

"I'll indulge you, Mr. Kaplan, but there's a limit."

"Nouriel. You can call me Nouriel."

At that, she got up from her chair and motioned for him to do likewise. She led him away from her desk to a small round conference table where the two sat down. The table was situated in front of a huge glass window through which one could see a vast panorama of skyscrapers with similar windows, each reflecting the light of the afternoon sun.

"All right, Nouriel. Tell me about your mystery."

"It's not *my* mystery. It's much bigger than me. You have no idea how big, or what it involves."

"And what does it involve?"

"Everything. It involves everything, and it explains everything…everything that's happened, that's happening, and everything that's going to happen."

"What do you mean?"

"Behind September 11…"

"How could an ancient mystery possibly have anything to do with September 11?"

"An ancient mystery behind everything from 9/11 to the economy…to the housing boom…to the war in Iraq…to the collapse of Wall Street. Everything in precise detail."

"How? How could an ancient mystery possibly…"

"Affect your life? Your bank account? Your future? But it does. And it holds the key to America's future…to the rise and fall of nations…to world history. And it's not only a mystery, it's a message, an alarm."

"An alarm?" she asked. "An alarm of what?"

"Of warning."

"To whom?"

"America."

"Why?"

"When you hear it," he said, "you'll understand why."

"All this from a mystery that goes back…how far did you say?"

"I didn't say."

"So how far back does it go?"

"Two and a half thousand years."

"A two-and-a-half-thousand-year-old mystery behind what's happening in the twenty-first century from politics to the economy to foreign affairs—all that and you're the only one who knows about it?"

"I'm not the only one."

"Who else knows about it?" she asked.

"There's at least one other."

"Not the government? The government has no idea, even though it's behind all that?"

"As far as I know, no government, no intelligence agency, no one else."

"No one but you."

"And at least one other."

"And how did you happen to discover it?"

"I didn't discover it," he answered. "It was given to me."

"Given? By whom?"

"A man."

"And who was this man?"

"It's hard to say."

At this she leaned forward and spoke to him in a tone both intense and slightly sarcastic.

"Try me," she said.

"You won't understand."

"What was his name?"

"I don't know."

"You don't know?" she replied, with a trace of amusement in her voice.

"No, he never told me."

"So this earth-shattering mystery is known only by you and this one man who gave it to you but doesn't have a name."

"I didn't say he didn't have a name. He just never told it to me."

"And you never asked?"

"I did, but he never told me."

"No phone number?"

"He never gave me one."

"No business card?"

"No."

"Not even an e-mail?"

"I don't expect you to believe me yet."

"Why not?" she replied, making no attempt to hide her skepticism. "It sounds so plausible!"

"But hear me out."

"So this man with no name gives you this mystery."

"That's correct."

"And why to you?"

"I guess I was the right one."

"So you were chosen?"

"I guess so," he replied, his voice trailing off.

"And where did *he* get the mystery from?"

"I don't know."

"A mystery on which the nation's future is hanging, and no one knows where it came from?"

"From where do prophets get their messages?"

"Prophets!" she said. "So now we're talking prophets?"

"I guess we are."

"As in Isaiah…Jeremiah?"

"Something like that."

"The last time I heard about prophets I was in Sunday school, Nouriel. Prophets don't exist anymore. They've been gone for ages."

"How do you know?"

"So you're telling me that the man who gave you this revelation is a prophet?"

"Something like that."

"He told you he was a prophet?"

"No. He never came out and said it."

"And you believe all this because it came from a prophet?"

"No," he answered. "It wouldn't have mattered who said it. It's not about the messenger; it's about the message."

"So why are you telling *me* all this? Why did you come here? I'm not exactly known for dealing with anything remotely like this."

"Because the stakes are so high. Because the future is hanging on it. Because it affects millions of people."

"And you think I have a part in this?"

"I do."

"Really?"

"Yes."

She leaned back in her chair and stared at him for a moment, intrigued, amused, and still trying to figure him out.

"So, Nouriel, tell me how it all began."

He reached into his coat pocket, laid his closed hand down on the table, then opened it. In the middle of his palm was a small object of reddish, golden-brown clay, circular and about two inches in diameter.

"It all began with this."

He handed it to her. She began examining it. The more she looked at it, the more intrigued she became. It was covered with what appeared to be ancient inscriptions.

"It all began with this."

"And what is it?"

"It's a seal," he answered. "It's the first seal."

Chapter 2

The Prophet

אֵ חָ

A SEAL," SHE REPEATED as she continued her examination of the object in her hands. "And what exactly is a seal?"

"It's what they used in ancient times to mark a document as authentic or authoritative."

She laid it down on the table.

"And the markings?"

"Letters," he said, "Paleo-Hebrew engravings."

"Paleo-Hebrew...I've never heard of it."

"It's an ancient form of Hebrew script."

"Are you some kind of an archaeologist?"

"No," he replied, "a journalist, a freelance journalist."

"Wait a minute...Kaplan...Nouriel Kaplan. I knew the name was familiar. You've done pieces in magazines and on the Internet."

"Guilty."

"Why didn't it hit me before?" She shook her head back and forth in her amazement over not having recognized the name at the start. "So you're *not* crazy after all," she said, almost apologetically.

"Some would disagree with such a presumption," he answered. At that, her demeanor and tone became markedly less guarded.

"But this has to be a departure for you. How did you get involved with it?"

"This is how," he said, lifting the clay seal from the table. "This is what began everything."

"How did you get it?"

"Believe it or not, it came in the mail."

"You ordered it?"

"No. I didn't order it, and I wasn't expecting it. It just came...a small brown package with my name and address and no return address. Inside was this ancient-looking seal, nothing else, no letter of explanation...nothing."

"And what did you think?"

"I didn't know what to think. What was I supposed to make of it? It had no connection to anything in my life. Who would have sent it to me with no explanation? I put it away. But it continued to intrigue me. One day...it was late afternoon...I found myself unable to stop thinking about it. I decided to go outside for some fresh air. I put the seal in my coat pocket and went for a walk along the Hudson River. It was a windy day. The sky was dark, filled with ominous-looking clouds. After some time I sat down on one of the benches overlooking the water. I took out the seal and began examining it. I wasn't alone on the bench; there was a man sitting to my left."

◆◆◆

"Looks like a storm," he said without turning to me or interrupting his gaze, which was fixed on the sky above the water.

"It does," I replied.

That's when he decided to look, first at me and then at the seal in my hand. And that's when the intensity of his gaze first struck me. "What's that?" he asked.

"Some archaeological artifact."

"May I see it?" he said. "I promise to be careful."

I was reluctant, but for some reason...thinking back, I don't know exactly why, I agreed to his request. He began examining its details.

"Do you have any idea what it is?" I asked.

"Where did you get it?"

"Why?"

"It's very interesting. It's an ancient seal."

"Which is what?"

He continued, "Seals like this one were used to mark important documents—edicts, decrees, communications by kings, rulers, princes, priests, and scribes—in ancient times. The seal was the sign of authenticity. It would let you know that the message was real, from someone important, and to be taken seriously."

"What about the writing?"

"It's in ancient Paleo-Hebrew, from…I would say…the sixth to seventh century B.C. How did you get it?"

"Someone sent it to me."

"Who?"

"I don't know."

He removed his gaze from the object just long enough to make eye contact with me as if surprised by my response.

"You don't know who sent it to you?"

"No."

"Someone just sent you this in the mail."

"How do you know so much about it?"

"About seals?"

"Yes."

"Ancient objects are a hobby of mine. It's Judean."

"Judean?"

"The seal is from the kingdom of Judah."

"And that's significant?"

"Very. It's where most of the Bible came from, the kingdom of Judah—Israel. There was never a people for whom the authenticity of a written word meant so much. For them, it was a matter of life or death. You see, God spoke to them. He sent them words, prophetic messages of correction. Messages to save them from calamity. If they ignored such a message, the result would be catastrophic."

"And God sent these words how?"

"Through His messengers, through His servants, the prophets."

"And how exactly would He *send* these messages?"

"The prophet would receive the word through impartation—a vision, a dream, an utterance, a sign. He would then be responsible to deliver the word to the nation, either by proclaiming it or by committing it to writing or by performing a prophetic act."

"And how would the nation know if a word came from God or

not…if it was authentic? How would you recognize an authentic prophet?"

"It wouldn't be by his appearance," he said, "if that's what you mean. He wouldn't necessarily look any different from anyone else, except that he was *called*. He could be a prince or a farmer, a shepherd, a carpenter. He could be sitting right next to you, and you'd have no idea you were sitting next to a prophet. It wasn't about the prophet but about the One who sent him."

"So then how would they know if the message was from God?"

"It would contain the mark, the fingerprint of the One who sent it."

"Like a seal."

"Yes, like a seal…and the word would come at the appointed time—when the nation needed to hear it, in critical times and in times of apostasy and danger."

"Danger?"

"Of judgment," he replied.

"And would they listen to the prophets?"

"Some would; most would not. They preferred to hear pleasant messages. But the messages of the prophets weren't meant to make them feel good but to warn them. So the prophets were persecuted…and then came judgment…calamity…destruction." He handed me back the seal.

———◆◆◆———

"It was him," said Ana, breaking her silence. "The man on the bench…he was the prophet."

"Yes."

"He was letting you know that when he said, 'He could be sitting right next to you.'"

"Exactly."

"What did he look like?"

"Somewhat thin, dark hair, a closely cropped beard. He was Mediterranean or Middle Eastern looking."

"And what was he wearing?"

"A long dark coat. He was always wearing the same coat every time I saw him."

"So he handed you back the seal."

"Yes, and I asked him, 'So why would anyone want to send me an ancient seal?'

"'A seal,' he said, 'bears witness to a message that it's authentic or that it's of great importance.'

"'But what would that have to do with me?' I asked. 'I don't have anything to do with messages of great importance.'

"'Maybe you do and just don't know it.'

"'You're very mystical, you know.'

"'Or maybe,' he said, 'you're about to receive one.'

"'What do you mean?'

"'A message of great importance,' he replied. His left hand had been resting on his lap for the entire length of the conversation... closed. That's when he opened it. In the middle of his palm was a seal."

"No!" said Ana, now leaning forward in her chair. "How could he have?"

"But he did."

"...a seal like yours?"

"Like mine, except with different markings."

"But how did he...?"

"Exactly. That's what *I* wanted to know."

◆◆◆

I couldn't think straight. I couldn't process it. My heart was pounding, and my voice grew tense. "What's that?" I asked. I knew what it was, but I didn't know how else to say it.

"A seal," he replied.

"What I meant was, what are you doing with a seal?"

"What am *I* doing with a seal? The question is, 'What are *you* doing with a seal?'"

"How did you get that?" I countered.

"I told you, it's my hobby. I collect them."

"You collect seals?"

"Yes."

"*You're* the one!" I said, my voice filled with tension and rising. "You're the one behind it. You're the one who sent it to me. What is this all about?"

"It's all about finding out what it's all about."

"How did you do this? How did you manage to... You've been following me?"

"Following *you*? I was the one sitting on the bench. *You're* the one who came after. Are you sure *you* weren't following *me*?"

"I don't even know you."

"Nevertheless, you were the one who came after."

He was right, of course. He couldn't have been following me. He was already there. *I* was the one who sat down next to him. And yet in his hand was a seal just like the one in mine, as if he knew I would come, as if he'd been waiting. But it was a rare thing for me to go there. It wasn't planned. And *I* was the one who chose to sit down at that particular bench and to take out the seal at that particular moment. I asked him again, "What is this all about?"

"You've been given a seal," he said, "Where there's a seal, there must be a message. Do you have a message?"

"No," I replied, almost defensively, "I don't have any message."

At that he paused and just stared for a few moments into the distance. Then he turned to me and, looking directly into my eyes, uttered his reply. "But *I* do."

"What do you mean?" I asked.

"But I do have a message."

"What message?"

"I have a message... for you."

At that point I was almost shaking. I got up from the bench. "I don't think so," I said in a voice now tense with anxiety. "I have no idea how you managed to do this, but it has nothing to do with me."

"It's the time," he replied.

I wanted to run, but I couldn't. I was torn between two impulses— the urge to get as far away from that bench as I could and the need to hear what he had to say. I was frozen. And then he spoke again.

"It's the time, Nouriel."

"Nouriel!" I replied almost shouting, "How did you...?"

———— ♦♦♦ ————

"How could he have *possibly* known your name?" Ana interjected.

"A good question, but he never answered it. Instead, he turned his gaze back to the distance ahead and continued speaking. 'It's the appointed time, but not for an ancient nation. It's time for the word to be given... for the mystery to be revealed... for the message to go forth. It's the appointed time—but not for an ancient nation.'"

———— ♦♦♦ ————

"This has nothing to do with me," I said again.

"Then why were you given the seal?" he asked.

"Who *are* you?" I countered.

He didn't answer that but just looked at me. It was a silence as intense as anything else that took place that day. I couldn't stay there any longer.

———— ♦♦♦ ————

"So you left him?" she asked.

"Yes."

"And what did he do when you left?"

"I don't know. I didn't look back."

"So how did you make sense of all that?"

"I didn't. I went home. But I couldn't stop thinking about it. For days it was almost impossible to sleep. I picked up a Bible to look for anything I could find on the prophets and their messages. Days went by, weeks, and I could hardly think of anything but that encounter. And then I returned."

"To the bench by the Hudson."

"Yes, but not exactly *to* the bench, but near it, to where I could see it from a distance."

"Why?"

"Because I wasn't sure I wanted to see him again."

"But you *did* want to see him again."

"Again, I was torn. I knew that if I didn't see him again, I'd never know the answer. At the same time I was afraid of what that might mean. And yet, still I was drawn back. I had to return."

"And…?"

"And he wasn't there. I returned a second time. And again he wasn't there. And then a third time."

"And…?"

"The third time he was there just as he was the first time, sitting on the same bench on the same spot, in the same long dark coat."

"And…?"

"And then it began."

Chapter 3

Kingdom's Eve and the Nine Harbingers

א ה

I WAS STANDING BEHIND the bench and to the right.

"You returned," said the prophet, without any movement of his head, but still maintaining his gaze into the distance. He couldn't possibly have seen me, but he knew I was there. It was something I could never get used to ... being with someone you felt could, at any given time, see through you.

"Why?" he asked, still gazing toward the waters. "Why did you return?"

"Because," I replied, "you're the only one who can give me the answer."

"To what?" he asked.

"To the problem."

"To what problem?"

"To the problem of you."

"I'm the only one who can answer the problem of me?" he said with a hint of playfulness in his voice. "I don't know, Nouriel; it sounds like a paradox to me."

"Am I wrong?" I asked.

"No," he replied. "You're not wrong."

I joined him on the bench. It was only then that he broke his gaze to look at me. "But are you ready?" he asked.

"For ...?"

"The answer."

"I hope so."

"Then let's begin. You're a journalist; did you bring a notepad or a recording device?"

"A recording device."

"Good," he said. "I thought you would have. Turn it on."

I removed the recorder from my coat pocket and pressed *record*. From then on I was even more careful to make sure I never went anywhere without it, just in case.

◆◆◆

"So then everything the prophet said, you recorded?" asked Ana.

"Virtually everything."

"*Recordings of the Prophet*...not a bad title for a book."

"As soon as I turned it on, he returned his gaze back to the waters and slightly upward, focusing on no particular object as far as I could see. Then he began to speak as if recalling some distant memory."

◆◆◆

"They had no idea what was coming. They thought it would all go on as it always had, as if it would never change. They had no idea what was about to happen or what it was all leading to. Everything they had ever known, up to that point, their entire world, would vanish."

"Who?"

"An ancient people...an ancient kingdom. Israel, the northern kingdom, eighth century B.C. They should have known. It was all there from the beginning, but they forgot."

"Forgot what?"

"Their purpose, their foundation, that which made them unique. No other nation had been called into being for the will of God or dedicated to His purposes from conception. No other people had been given a covenant. But the covenant had a condition. If they followed the ways of God, they would become the most blessed of nations. But if they fell away and turned against His ways, then their blessings would be removed and replaced by calamity, as they did, and as it was."

"But why would they turn away if they were given so much?"

"It's a mystery," said the prophet, "a kind of spiritual amnesia. When it began, they were still using God's name, but with less and less meaning behind it. Then they started merging Him, confusing Him with the gods of the nations. And then they began turning against Him—subtly at first, then outright, then brazenly—driving Him out of their national life and bringing in idols to fill the void. The land became covered with idols and altars to foreign gods. They rejected their covenant, abandoned their standards, and exchanged the values they had always lived by for those they had never known— spirituality for sensuality, holiness for profanity, and righteousness for self-interest. They cut themselves off from the faith on which their nation had been established and became strangers to God. And as for their most innocent, their little children, they offered them up as sacrifices."

"Literally?" I asked. "They literally killed their own children?"

"On the altars of Baal and Molech, their newfound gods. That's how far they descended. Everything was now upside down. What they had once known as right, they now saw as outdated, intolerant, and immoral. And what they had once known as immoral, they now championed and celebrated as sacred. They had transformed themselves into the enemies of the God they had once worshiped and the faith they had once followed, until the very mention of His name was banned from their public squares. And yet in spite of all this, He was merciful and called to them, again and again."

"Through the prophets?"

"Through the prophets—Elijah, Elisha, Hosea, and Amos, pleading with them, warning them, calling them to return. But they rejected the call and declared war on those who remained faithful. They branded them as troublemakers, irritants, dangerous, and, finally, enemies of the state. They were marginalized, vilified, persecuted, and even hunted down. So the nation grew deaf to the call of those trying to save them from judgment. The alarm would have to grow louder and the warnings more severe."

"More severe?"

"They would enter a new stage. The words of the prophets would now be joined to the sound of calamity. God would remove the hedge."

"Remove what hedge?" I asked.

"The hedge He had placed around them, the hedge of protection, of national security that had kept them safe up to that point. As long as it was in place, they were safe. No enemy kingdom, no empire, no power on earth could touch them. But once it was removed, everything changed. Their enemies could now enter, breach their land, and enter their gates. It was a new phase, much more dangerous than before. Thus began the days of calamities and shakings...the days of final warning."

"And when did this all happen? When was this hedge removed?"

"732 B.C."

"Maybe I'm missing something," I said. "But what does all this, what happened two and a half thousand years ago, have to do with anything...with now? What does it have to do with why you're here and why I'm listening to all this? When we first met, you said it wasn't about an ancient nation. But so far all you've talked about is an ancient nation."

"I said, 'Not *for* an ancient nation.' That's different."

"But why are you talking about an ancient nation?"

"Because unless you understand what happened then, you'll never understand what's happening now."

"Now? So it's some kind of key?"

"A key for the appointed time, for the word to be given and for the message to go forth, but not for an ancient nation."

"Then for what...for what nation?"

He was silent.

I asked him again, "Then for what nation?"

It was only then that he voiced it.

"America," he said. "Now for America."

With that, he got up from the bench and walked over toward the water.

I couldn't let it go at that. I followed him there. "All this has to do with America?"

"Yes."

"So it's the *appointed time* for America? For a mystery to be revealed and a message to be given to America?"

"Yes."

"But what does America have to do with ancient Israel?"

"Israel was unique among nations in that it was conceived and dedicated at its foundation for the purposes of God."

"OK…"

"But there was one other—a civilization also conceived and dedicated to the will of God from its conception…America. In fact, those who laid its foundations…"

"The Founding Fathers."

"No, long before the Founding Fathers. Those who laid America's foundations saw it as a new Israel, an Israel of the New World. And as with ancient Israel, they saw it as in covenant with God."

"Meaning?"

"Meaning its rise or fall would be dependent on its relationship with God. If it followed His ways, America would become the most blessed, prosperous, and powerful nation on earth. From the very beginning they foretold it. And what they foretold would come true. America would rise to heights no other nation had ever known. Not that it was ever without fault or sin, but it would aspire to fulfill its calling."

"What calling?"

"To be a vessel of redemption, an instrument of God's purposes, a light to the world. It would give refuge to the world's poor and needy, and hope to its oppressed. It would stand against tyranny. It would fight, more than once, against the dark movements of the modern world that threatened to engulf the earth. It would liberate millions. And, as much as it fulfilled its calling or aspired to, it would become the most blessed, the most prosperous, the most powerful, and the most revered nation on the earth—just as its founders had prophesied."

"But there's a *but* coming, isn't there?"

"Yes," he replied. "There was always another side to the covenant. If ancient Israel fell away from God and turned against His ways, its blessings would be removed and replaced with curses."

"But wasn't Israel surrounded by nations far worse," I asked, "with no concept of God or moral code? So why would Israel be judged?"

"Because to whom much is given, much is required. And no nation had ever been given so much. None had been so spiritually blessed. So the standards were higher, the stakes greater, and the judgment, when it came, more severe."

"And America..." I said.

"And America has done much good. And there's no shortage of nations far exceeding any of its faults or sins. But no nation in the modern world has ever been given so much. None has been so blessed. To whom much is given, much is required. If a nation so blessed by God should turn away from Him, what then?"

"Its blessings will be replaced with curses?"

"Yes."

"And has America turned away from God?" I asked.

"It has turned, and is turning."

"How?"

"In the same way Israel turned. It started with a spiritual complacency, then spiritual confusion, then the merging of God with idols, and then, ultimately, the rejection of His ways. Just as with ancient Israel, America began ruling God out of its life, turning, step by step, against His ways, at first subtly, and then, more and more, brazenly."

"When?" I asked. "When did it start?"

"There's no one simple answer. In America's greatest moments there was always sin, and in its worst moments, greatness. But there are critical junctures. In the middle of the twentieth century America began officially removing God from its national life. It abolished prayer and Scripture in its public schools. As ancient Israel had removed the Ten Commandments from its national consciousness, so America did likewise, removing the Ten Commandments from public view, banning it from its public squares, and taking it down, by government decree, from its walls. As it was in ancient Israel, so too in America, God was progressively driven out of the nation's public life. The very mention of the name God or Jesus in any relevant context became more and more taboo and unwelcome unless for the purpose of mockery and attack. That which had once been revered as sacred was now increasingly treated as profanity. And as God was driven out, idols were brought in to replace Him."

"But Americans don't worship idols."

"No," said the prophet, "they just don't call them *idols*. As God was expunged from American life, idols came in to fill the void—idols of sensuality, idols of greed, of money, success, comfort, materialism, pleasure, sexual immorality, self-worship, self-obsession. The sacred increasingly disappeared, and the profane took its place. It was another kind of spiritual amnesia; the nation forgot its foundations, its purpose, and its calling. The standards and values it had long upheld were now abandoned. What it had once known as immoral, it now accepted. Its culture was increasingly corrupted by the corrosion of sexual immorality, growing continuously more crude and vulgar. A wave of pornography began penetrating its media. The same nation that had once been dedicated to spreading God's light to the nations now filled the world with the pornographic and the obscene."

"Some would call it *tolerance*," I said.

"Yes," he replied, "the same tolerance that overtook ancient Israel…a tolerance for everything opposed to God, a growing tolerance for immorality and a growing intolerance for the pure—a tolerance that mocked, marginalized, and condemned those who remained faithful to the values now being discarded. Innocence was ridiculed and virtue was vilified. Children were taught of sexual immorality in public schools while the Word of God was banned. It was a tolerance that put the profane on public display and removed nativity scenes from public sight…contraband, as if somehow they had become a threat—a strangely intolerant tolerance."

"But still," I countered, "how does all that compare to what happened in ancient Israel? America doesn't offer its children on altars of sacrifice?"

"Does it not?" he said. "Ten years after removing prayer and Scripture from its public schools, the nation legalized the killing of its unborn. The blood of the innocent now stained its collective hands. Israel had sacrificed thousands on the altars of Baal and Molech. But by the dawn of the twenty-first century, America had sacrificed *millions*. For its thousands, judgment came upon Israel. What then of America?"

"So what are you saying?

He didn't respond.

"Is America in danger of judgment?" I asked.

Again he was silent.

"Tell me…is America in danger of judgment?"

"Are you sure you want to know the answer?"

"I'm sure."

"The answer to your question is *yes*…Yes. America is in danger of judgment."

I didn't respond immediately. I was trying to come up with a defense. Finally I said, "It can't be as bad as it was in ancient Israel. They came against the prophets. But if God sent a message today to America, calling it back, people would listen."

"Would they?"

"They wouldn't?"

"No."

"How do you know?"

"Because they've deafened their ears to those voices. So as with ancient Israel, the alarm would have to grow louder and the calling more severe."

"Which means what?"

"Which means that America would enter a new stage."

"Of what?"

"Of what happened to Israel," he answered.

"The hedge?"

"The removal of the nation's hedge of protection."

"And what would it mean if something like that would happen?" There was a long pause before he answered that. "It already has."

"What do you mean?"

"America's hedge has already been removed, and the Nine Harbingers have been manifested."

"The Nine Harbingers?"

"The Nine Harbingers that manifested in ancient Israel in the nation's last days. Each one was a sign. Each one was a warning of judgment...of their end...the Nine Harbingers of judgment."

"I don't understand."

"It's all happening again according to the same pattern, according to the judgment of ancient Israel. The Nine Harbingers that appeared in the last days of ancient Israel are now appearing in America."

"Appearing in America?"

"Each one manifesting on American soil. Each one containing a prophetic message. And upon these, the future of the nation hangs."

"I don't understand..."

"You don't have to understand. It will all be revealed."

He asked me if I had the seal. I did. I removed it from my pocket and handed it to him. He then opened up his other hand to reveal another seal, the same one he was holding the day we met. He placed it in my hand. "Nine seals, one for each Harbinger, one for each mystery."

"And this one?" I asked.

"This is the seal of the First Harbinger."

"And the one I gave you?"

"That was *your* seal. But as for the seals of the Harbingers, there are eight more. You'll keep each seal until we meet again, at which time you'll return it to me to receive the next seal and the next revelation. You'll only have one seal at a time, the security deposit of a coming mystery."

"And you trust me to give it back to you?" I asked.

"Yes."

"But how do you know you'll ever see me again?"

"You're the one seeking, and you won't stop until you find. In any case, I have my own security deposit, don't I?"

He paused and then slightly nodding his head said, "Until then, Nouriel." And he began to walk away.

"And *my* seal?" I shouted after him.

"You'll get it back when we're finished," he replied without stopping or turning his head"

"And when will we meet again?" I asked.

"When it's time to speak of the First Harbinger."

"Here?"

"At the appointed place," he replied.

"How will I know?"

"How did you know to come here in the first place?" he asked

"I didn't."

"So you won't know again, and yet you'll be there."

And then he was gone.

Chapter 4

The First Harbinger: The Breach

ⁿ ℵ

B<small>UT YOU DID</small> see the prophet after that?"

"Yes."

"And you didn't have *any* contact with him before you saw him again?"

"That's right."

"I don't understand," she said. "How did you know where to meet him or when...if he never told you?

"I didn't know where or when," he replied. "We just met."

"I still don't get it."

"It would just happen. Sometimes I'd be led by the clues, and sometimes I'd be led in spite of them. Even when I got them wrong I'd still end up in the right place, eventually. And sometimes, even with no clues, when I wasn't even searching...it would still happen. We just ended up in the same place. Call it *predestination*. I don't know. It just happened."

"Why do you think the prophet gave you clues to put together instead of just telling you from the start?"

"I don't know. Maybe because it was the process of trying to put it all together that led to the next encounter. I think it was also so that each Harbinger would be burned into my consciousness."

"So you met him again. And what happened? No, wait a minute." She got up from the table, walked over to her desk, and pressed one of the buttons on her phone set. "Hold off any incoming calls," she said. "Don't allow any interruptions."

"Even the calls that are scheduled?" replied a woman's voice on the speaker phone.

"Yes. Tell them something came up and that I'll get back as soon as possible. Apologize for me…warmly."

"For how long?"

"I don't know," she said, "for the rest of the day." She returned to the table and refocused her attention. "OK, so you met him again," she said. "When and where?"

"It was weeks after our last encounter. During that time I studied the seal looking for clues to the mystery of the First Harbinger."

"And what was on it?"

"Markings and shapes, but one that was clearly the central image and the largest. It was…how can I describe it? There was a horizontal line as if it was the top border of some object or structure. The line dipped down in the middle of the seal, then back up again, then continued as a horizontal line to the other side. So it formed something like a V in the middle. I couldn't make anything out of it."

"So?"

"So I went back to the bench by the water. But he wasn't there. I went back several more times after that, but nothing. More weeks went by, and then months. I wondered if I'd ever see him again. And the whole thing still didn't seem real. I would have almost doubted my memory if it wasn't for the seal. One day…it was a Tuesday morning, I was in Lower Manhattan, the very bottom of the island, in Battery Park, pondering the words of the prophet, and looking across the waters at the Statue of Liberty in the distance.

◆◆◆

At first I didn't notice it, a dark figure standing about fifty feet in front of me and to the right. It was him. He was also facing the water, so I could only see his back. Whether he was looking at the statue or at some other object or just at the water, I don't know. He turned to the side, just for a moment. That's when I recognized him. I made my way over to him as fast as I could, not wanting to risk missing the moment. While I was still in back of him, he spoke…again, without breaking his gaze, at least at first.

"Nouriel," he said.

"Present," I replied.

"And just on time."

"Did you arrange that too?" I asked.

"No. Have you studied the seal?"

"I have."

"And what did you find?"

"Nothing."

"Did you bring your recorder?"

"It's always with me."

"Then let's begin," he said, turning to gaze toward me for the first time in the exchange. A warm breeze ruffled his hair as he spoke above the sound of seagulls in the background. "Take out the seal," he said. "What do you see?"

"Inscriptions, symbols, and one main symbol."

"What do you make of it?"

"I don't know. It's something like a V."

"It's an image, Nouriel."

"Of what?"

"The top of a wall," he said. "It's a wall of protection."

"And what's the V in the middle?"

"Not a V," he replied, "a breach."

"A breach?"

"A gap—a break, an opening in the wall. The wall is broken, the sign that an enemy has entered in."

"It's the removing of the hedge of protection. It's what happened to ancient Israel?"

"Yes. With no other way of getting through to them, the hedge of protection is removed. The year is 732 B.C. Israel's enemies invade the land and wreak havoc. The calamity traumatizes the nation. But it takes place on a limited scale. The enemy strikes and then withdraws. It's a foreshadowing of something much greater and much more severe—a warning…a harbinger of a future judgment so great that if it ever came to pass, the nation would never recover."

"So the warning is the removal of the hedge."

"Yes," said the prophet, "a late-stage warning, allowed to take place only when nothing else would wake them up… limited…restrained…the sound of an alarm for the purpose of averting a much greater calamity. It never could have happened had Israel remained inside the will of God. No enemy could have ever breached its walls. But outside the will of God, any notion of national security or invincibility was an illusion. The breach exposed it. The nation was in danger. It would be shaken to its foundation…and apart from returning to God, there was no wall strong enough to protect them. It was their wake-up call."

"So they never woke up?"

"No," he replied. "Most would see the tragedy as a matter of defense, national security, or foreign policy. They committed themselves to making sure it would never happen again. They fortified their defenses, strengthened their walls, and formed strategic alliances. Few of them pondered the possibility that there could be any deeper significance behind it. And yet the voices of their prophets, the words of their Scriptures, and an uneasy stirring in their hearts were all warning them that something was wrong. The nation had departed from God. But apart from the prophets, few realized the critical line they had crossed and the new and dangerous era they had entered. No political or military power would be strong enough to ensure their safety; only a return to God. The attack was a warning and a harbinger of judgment."

"So what happened after they missed their wake-up call?"

"As time passed, it appeared as if life was gradually returning to normal. There was a respite, peace. With every passing year, it seemed as if the danger was farther behind them. But it was an illusion. The problem and the danger only increased. It was a period of grace, given to them in mercy, that they might change their course and avert the judgment. But if not, then a greater judgment would come, and that first breaching of their walls would be remembered as the harbinger that was the beginning of their fall. These were their most critical of days." He paused. "The seal, Nouriel…hand it to me."

So I gave it to him. He lifted it up in his right hand.

"The First Harbinger," he said, holding the seal level with my eyes. "The Breach. The nation that had long known blessing and security witnesses the failure of its defenses. Its walls of protection are broken through, its national security is breached, and its illusion of invincibility shattered. The days of the Harbingers begin."

"And this has something to do with America?" I asked.

"America was the most blessed nation on earth, its blessings shielded by a powerful hedge of national protection. As its founders had foretold, if the nation followed the ways of God, it would be blessed not only with prosperity and power but also with peace and security."

"But if America turned away from God, its protection would be removed?"

"Yes, and so it did. And so it was. Its hedge of protection was removed, and its walls were breached."

"Its walls were breached? When?" I asked.

The prophet was silent, as if waiting for me to say it, or waiting for it to hit me. And then it did...all at once.

"September 11!"

"Yes," said the prophet. "The First Harbinger, the Breach. The nation that had so long known the blessings of peace and security witnesses its walls of protection broken through as its defenses fail. On September 11, 2001, the walls of America's national security were breached. It happened right there," he said, pointing to the sky above the waters. "The second attack. That's how it came. The most powerful nation on earth and the most sophisticated defense system ever built by man..."

"Its wall of defense...breached."

"And then came the mistake," he said. "Then came the repeating of the ancient mistake. America responded to the calamity as if it were only a matter of security and defense...and nothing more. It would strengthen its national defenses and fortify its walls of protection. There was no pausing to ponder whether there could be anything of deeper significance behind it, no asking if something could be wrong, no searching of its ways."

"Was God behind it?" I asked.

"Man was behind it," he answered. "Evil men were behind it. Up to that point they had been restrained. But that restraint would have its limits. As with the attack on ancient Israel, an attack would now be allowed on American soil."

"But it was planned by evil men," I countered. "It was evil."

"Yes," he replied, "but God can cause that which is evil to work for good."

"But what good?"

"The sounding of an alarm to wake up a sleeping nation, to change its course, to save it from judgment."

"But then was God with America's enemies?"

"No. No more than He was with those who attacked ancient Israel. Those who do such things are His enemies as well. God was against those who attacked America and would deal with them just as He dealt with the enemies of ancient Israel."

"And what about those who perished?" I asked.

"When calamity came to ancient Israel, both the righteous and the unrighteous were touched by it. Both perished alike. The judgment was upon the nation. But that the innocent and righteous also perished in those calamities was not a matter of judgment but of sorrow. But for the nation, the fact that such calamities could have happened in the first place was a matter of both warning and judgment. Each took place in its own realm. So it was with 9/11; the calamity took place in two different realms—the private realm of individuals and the public realm of the nation. In the first realm is only sorrow, and the magnitude of the calamity is secondary. And for those touched by it, the loss of one life is the loss of an entire world. The charge here is to bind up the broken, to comfort, to support, and to never forget the wounded and the bereaved. But the second realm is distinct and separate, centering not on the individual but on the nation as a whole. It's in this second realm that the matter of judgment remains."

"It's hard to receive," I replied.

"Could you receive it from another?"

"What do you mean?"

"Abraham Lincoln."

"What does he have to do with…"

"Do you know how many lives were lost in the American Civil War?"

"I have no idea…thousands?"

"*Hundreds* of thousands. And Lincoln spoke of the calamity devastating the nation as the judgment of a righteous God—not on any individual but on the nation as a whole."

"But it's a hard…"

"Of course it is, as it was for Isaiah and Jeremiah and all the prophets and others who wept and cried out for their people. But if we fail to consider the possibility…if we avoid addressing the issue…do we not then become accountable for what follows?"

"For what follows? I don't know. But even to say, 'God allowed it to happen'…"

"It *happened*, Nouriel. Therefore it had to have been allowed to happen. That's not the question. Rather, the only question is whether it was allowed to happen for no reason or whether there was, within it, a redemptive purpose."

"On 9/11 people were asking, 'Where was God?'"

"Where was God?" he said, as if surprised by the question. "We drove Him out of our schools, out of our government, out of our media, out of our culture, out of our public square. We drove Him out of our national life, and then we ask, 'Where is God?'"

"Then He wasn't there?"

"Still, He was there. He was there with those who lost their loved ones and is still there to heal the broken and comfort those who mourn. He was there with those who gave their lives so others could live, shadows of Him. And He was there, as well, with all the countless others who would have perished that day if not for the countless turns of details and events that saved them. And for those who perished…those who were with God in life are now with Him in eternity. For these, it was not a day of national calamity but of release. He was with them and *is* with them."

"You said something about what happened in ancient Israel after the attack, that things began to return to normal."

"I spoke of things *appearing* to return to normal. There's a difference."

"So was the hedge of protection back in place?"

"To a degree and for a time. But the danger was still there."

"And what about America after 9/11?" I asked.

"In the months and years after 9/11 it appeared likewise as if things had returned to some state of normalcy. As time passed, as the initial shock wore off and the trauma lessened, there was a growing temptation to go on almost as if it had never happened, as if the nation were still somehow immune to destruction. So it was in the last days of ancient Israel. But it was all an illusion."

There was a long silence after that…broken only by the sound of the seagulls. Then he continued as if there had been no break. "It was all a fatal illusion. So then…what of America?"

◆◆◆

I didn't answer him. I don't believe he was expecting me to. After posing the question, he reached into his coat pocket to reveal another seal, which he placed into my hand.

"The Seal of the Second Harbinger," he said.

"And what did it look like?" asked Ana.

"Overall, like the others…except for the images…"

"Which were…"

"…figures."

"Of what?"

"Of men."

"What kind of men?"

"I had no idea. I tried to get him to tell me by asking, 'So what am I looking at?'"

"It's not so hard," he replied.

"Give me a clue…something."

"Until next time, Nouriel." And with that, he began to walk away.

"When…next time? Where?"

"The same time and place," he said, again without stopping to look back.

"Here?"

"No."

"Then where and when?"

"Wherever and whenever…just be sure to be there."

"At least give me a clue to help me unlock the seal."

"By the ruins of an ancient people."

"Is that the clue," I shouted after him, "or is that where we're supposed to meet?"

"Ah, but that would require another clue," he shouted back.

"*Another* clue. Then it *was* a clue about the Second Harbinger and not about where we're supposed to meet," I shouted back.

"Perhaps…and perhaps not," he replied.

He wasn't easy that way. But it was enough for me to begin searching for the meaning behind the Second Harbinger…a mystery to be found somewhere by the ruins of an ancient people.

Chapter 5

The Second Harbinger: The Terrorist

אה

THE FIGURES ON the seal, Nouriel...what did they look like?"
she asked.

"Men with beards, in robes and with some sort of head coverings.
Their beards were squarish and heavily stylized. Some were holding
bows and arrows and aiming them upward, all very ancient looking
and alien."

"So how did you unlock the mystery?"

"By the ruins of an ancient people, that was the clue. The figures
on the seal had to be the ancient people he referred to. That much
seemed obvious. But which ancient people? Who were they?"

"So what did you do?"

"The Metropolitan Museum...It's filled with artifacts of ancient
peoples, and it's enormous. So I figured that whoever these people
were, if they were of any historical significance, their artifacts
would be on display in that museum. I would go there with the
seal, hoping to find a match."

"And?"

"It was as impressive as I had hoped it would be, with artifacts
from Egypt, Rome, Greece, Persia, Babylon...I started with the
Egyptian wing on the first floor. But nothing matched. Then I
searched through the Greek and Roman wing. But again, no
matches. Then I made my way up the grand staircase and over to
the Department of Ancient Near Eastern Art. That's where I saw it.
It was impossible to miss. It was gigantic."

"What was gigantic?" she asked.

"Massive stone walls covered with reliefs of giant figures—
warriors, priests, and a number of creatures, part-human...part-bird,

composite creatures. I took out the seal and compared the figures to those on the wall. They were the same figures, the same squarish beards, the same clothing, and all in the same style of artwork and engraving. It was a match."

"An exact match?"

"It wasn't the same image," he replied, "but it was the same people, the same civilization."

"So who were they?"

"They were the ancient Assyrians."

"And what did you make of it?"

"I didn't have time to make anything of it. I was studying the images on the wall when I heard a voice from behind me."

---◆◆◆---

"Walls from the palace of Ashurnasirpal, king of Assyria."

I had assumed it was someone who worked for the museum or some other expert. I continued staring upward at the ancient figures.

"From the city of Nimrud, ninth century B.C.," the voice continued.

"Impressive," I said, not being able to contribute anything more informative or substantial to the conversation.

"The ruins of an ancient people," replied the voice.

---◆◆◆---

"With that, I knew it was him."

"And he knew you'd be there?"

"Either he knew I'd be there, or I was there and he happened to be there, or he was there and I happened to be there. I stopped trying to figure out how it worked. I turned around, and there was the prophet, standing in his long dark coat in the Department of Ancient Near Eastern Art. If you didn't know who he was, you wouldn't have noticed. He blended in. "

◆◆◆

"You go to museums?" I asked.

"Does that surprise you?" he answered. "Why wouldn't I?"

"I don't know. I just didn't picture you..."

"I told you it would be by the ruins of an ancient people. How many ruins of ancient peoples are there in New York City outside of museums? So what have you discovered?"

"It's the Assyrians. The ancient people are the Assyrians, and they have something to do with the Second Harbinger."

"Good, Nouriel. Now let's go deeper. What do you see?"

"What do you mean?"

"Look at them. How do they strike you?"

"Kind of stony."

"And what do you think lies behind their stoniness?"

"I have no idea."

And with that, and with an assurance one would expect from a museum tour guide, he began introducing me to the history of this ancient people. "They came from the mountainous regions of northern Mesopotamia. For centuries they lived in the shadows of stronger kingdoms. But at the dawn of the first millennium B.C., they began their rise to world power. They began their conquest of the surrounding lands and people. The Assyrians would march into Babylon, Syria, Lebanon, Persia, and Egypt until, at the peak of their power, most of the ancient Middle East was under their rule. So what kind of people do you think they were?"

"Militaristic?"

"With the largest army ever to stand on Mesopotamian soil up to that time. They devised new technologies of warfare—the moveable tower, the battering ram. Their empire was a war machine built on the subjugation of other nations and kingdoms. They were among the most brutal people ever to have walked the earth. The very mention of their name inspired dread throughout the ancient world."

"But why such dread?" I asked. "Other nations have been militaristic."

"One word," said the prophet. "*Terror.* The Assyrians made terror into a science. They systematized it, perfected it, and employed it as no other people or kingdom had ever done before. They burned cities to the ground, mutilated their prisoners, flayed alive those who rebelled against them, and nailed their skins to the wall for public display. The Assyrians were the masters of terror."

"And what do they have to do with the mystery?"

"It was the dark shadow of Assyrian terror that loomed over the kingdom of Israel. This was the danger against which the prophets warned. And it was only the hedge of God's protection that was keeping that danger at bay. But that was about to change. With the nation's descent into apostasy, it was no longer safe."

"It was the Assyrians," I said. "They were the ones who caused the breach."

"Correct," he replied. "In 732 B.C., with the nation's hedge of protection lifted, the Assyrians invaded the land of Israel."

"So that must have made it all the more terrifying for the people of Israel…that it was the Assyrians."

"Exactly. There couldn't have been any clearer warning of the coming judgment than that. And when, years later, Israel's final judgment came, the Assyrians would again be the means through which it would happen."

"But you're not saying that God was siding with the Assyrians?"

"Not in any way. This is the prophecy He gave concerning them:

"Woe to Assyria, the rod of My anger
And the staff in whose hand is My indignation.
I will send him against an ungodly nation.…
Yet he does not mean so,
Nor does his heart think so;
But it is in his heart to destroy,
And cut off not a few nations.[1]

"The Assyrians were the epitome of evil, and God was against them. The prophecy continued:

"I will punish the fruit of the arrogant heart of the king of Assyria, and the glory of his haughty looks...."

"Therefore the Lord, the Lord of hosts
Will send leanness among his fat one;
And under his glory
He will kindle a burning
Like the burning of a fire.[2]

"The Lord would bring the Assyrians into judgment. Their empire would vanish from the earth. But, for a time, in the days of Israel's apostasy, they would be allowed to breach its defenses and strike the land. If the Assyrian attack failed to awaken Israel from its spiritual stupor, then what could?"

It was then that he asked me for the seal. I placed it in his hand. He then began revealing its mystery. "The Second Harbinger," he said as he held up the seal so I could see the figures engraved on its face. "An enemy strikes the land. The attack is plotted out by the merciless and executed by the brutal, designed to traumatize the nation, to inflict shock and fear...terror...the sign of the Assyrian. The Second Harbinger: the Terrorist."

"The Assyrians were terrorists?" I asked.

"As much as any people have ever been. Terrorism is defined as: *the systematic application of terror, violence, and intimidation to achieve a specific end.* Terror as an applied science—this was the dark gift the Assyrians gave to the world."

We began walking along the stone reliefs, continuing our conversation while gazing up at the ancient figures above our heads.

"From the temples of Nineveh to the beer halls of Weimar Germany...to the barren caves of Afghanistan...from Sennacherib to Osama bin Laden...it all goes back to ancient Assyria. The Assyrians are the fathers of terrorism, and those who mercilessly plotted out the calamity on 9/11 were their spiritual children, another link in the mystery joining America to ancient Israel. In both cases, the warning began with a manifestation of terrorism."

"Did the 9/11 terrorists see themselves as modern-day Assyrians?"

"It doesn't matter," said the prophet. "That's what they were. Remember the prophecy against Assyria: '*It is in his heart to destroy.*'"

"Osama bin Laden."

"'*And cut off not a few nations.*'"

"That was his intention."

"But God would judge the Assyrians and their king."

"Then all those responsible for 9/11 are under His judgment?"

"'*I will punish the fruit of the arrogant heart of the king of Assyria,*'" said the prophet. "Yes, they are under His judgment. And the Lord will send *leanness* or devastation among his warriors."

"So the Assyrians are the spiritual fathers of al Qaeda."

"Yes, and not only the spiritual," he replied.

"And what does that mean?"

"The Assyrians were children of the Middle East, so too the terrorists of 9/11. The Assyrians were a Semitic people, so too the terrorists. The Assyrians spoke a language called *Akkadian*. The tongue is long extinct, but there is still spoken in the modern world one language considered to be the closest of all tongues to ancient Akkadian."

"Which is…?"

"Arabic."

"Arabic—the tongue of al Qaeda and the 9/11 terrorists."

"Yes, and so when the leaders of al Qaeda plotted their attack on America, and as the terrorists communicated with each other on 9/11 to carry it out, they did so using words and speech patterns that mirrored those used by the Assyrian leaders and warriors as they planned and executed their attack on Israel two and half thousand years earlier in 732 B.C."

"Like an ancient drama replaying itself in the modern world."

He didn't reply. We continued walking along the stone reliefs. It was strange. As I stared up at the ancient stone figures, I began to feel a sense of loathing toward them on one hand and some kind of dread on the other.

"The Assyrian invasion," said the prophet, "would ultimately draw ancient Israel into military conflict, war, and a final and tragic national drama. So too the attack of 9/11 would draw America into military conflict—a global battle against terrorism, encompassing a war in Afghanistan and another in Iraq. In the first war, the connection to 9/11 was clear. But in the second, it was not so clear. And yet there *was* a connection, but of a more mystical nature."

"What do you mean?"

"In April 2003, American soldiers would enter the Iraqi city of Mosul. Mosul would become one of America's major operational bases in the Iraqi war. Inside the city, near the junction of the Tigris and Khosr Rivers, there rest two mounds of earth. One is called *Kouyunjik*, the other *Nabi Yunus*. Hidden inside these mounds are the ruins of a once great civilization. The ruins are all that's left of the ancient city called *Nineveh*. Nineveh was the capital, the final resting place, and the graveyard of the Assyrian Empire."

"Assyria is *Iraq*?"

"It's the same land."

"The nation under judgment…is drawn into conflict with the land of Assyria…ancient Israel…now America."

"And American troops were now walking the same earth on which the feet of Assyrian soldiers had once marched. And among those watching them pass by were those who could still claim to be the descendants of the ancient Assyrians."

"Their actual flesh-and-blood descendants?" I asked.

"Yes," he replied. "And who knows but that the veins of the 9/11 terrorists did not also flow with the blood of the ancient Assyrians?"

"So ancient Israel, in its time of judgment, was drawn into war with Assyria, which is now Iraq."

"Yes," he answered.

"And now America was drawn into a war with the land of Assyria—Iraq."

"But Israel would ultimately discover that the danger it faced could not be solved by the power of its weapons or the thickness of its walls. The real danger was not *outside* its gates but *within* them. When the nation turned from God, it lost its protective covering. Apart from a return to God there would be no safety. But by the time they realized it, it would be too late. The chance was lost."

He stopped walking and pointed upward to the figure above him on the relief…a giant Assyrian archer.

"And now, the same sign that signaled the judgment of ancient Israel two and half thousand years before reappears in the modern world—no less dark and no less threatening—the sign of the Assyrian, the attack of the Terrorist."

"And what does it mean for America?" I asked.

"That *is* the question," he replied, "isn't it?"

With those words I sensed that our meeting was drawing to a close. And I was right. He handed me the next seal—the seal of the Third Harbinger.

"And what was on it?" she asked.

"Shapes…unrecognizable shapes."

"This one may be a bit more challenging for you," said the prophet in a voice conveying both caution and sympathy.

"So help me out," I replied.

"A word," he said.

"What do you mean?"

"You'll need a word to decode it."

"What kind of word?"

"The word that you need."

"Do you enjoy being so mysterious?" I asked.

"It's not a matter of enjoyment," he explained. "It's the nature of the job."

"Do you realize you've never even given me your name?"

"Would that make a difference, Nouriel?"

"No, I guess not. But shouldn't a journalist know who his source is?"

"And you don't know who your source is?" he asked.

I didn't answer. I suspected it was a loaded question. He resumed his studying of the ancient figures on the stone relief. I did likewise, but not for long. When I turned again to ask him for something more to go on, he was gone. I looked around in every direction, but there was no sign of him. I was alone again…just me and the Assyrians…in whose presence I was growing increasingly uncomfortable. I left the museum in search of the Third Harbinger. But it would be a search that would lead me to far more than I was expecting.

"What you do mean?" she asked.

"It would lead me to the key that would unlock the mystery of *all* the Harbingers."

Chapter 6

The Oracle

א ה

I COULDN'T MAKE ANY sense of what was on the seal. It was some sort of composite shape...mostly rectangles...joined together in a chaotic jumble. I decided instead to focus on the clue."

"On the word?" she asked.

"Yes."

"Pretty vague for a clue."

"Yes, but it was the only other thing I had to go on. So where do you find words?"

"In a book?"

"And where do you find books?"

"In a library?"

"So my search took me to the library, the New York Public Library, the one with the two stone lions standing guard outside and millions of books and resource materials inside. I was there virtually every day for weeks, going on any lead I could think of, searching for anything that would match the puzzling image on the seal.

"And did you find something?"

"No. But one day I was searching through a book of symbols in the Main Reading Room, sitting on a wooden chair against one of the library's long wooden tables by the light of a reading lamp, under a massive window and a chandelier. I took a break to look up from the page, and there he was."

"The prophet?"

"Sitting on the other side of the table, directly across from me. Silent...just watching me. I had been so engrossed in the book I never saw him sit down."

◆◆◆

"How long have you been here?" I asked.

"A few minutes."

"Why didn't you say something?"

"I was waiting."

"So this is the place of our next meeting. I wasn't sure I was on the right track."

"You're not," he replied. "And this is *not* the place of our next meeting."

"If this isn't the place of our next meeting, then why are you here?" I countered. "And why am *I* here? And why are we meeting?"

"I would call this *an intervention*. I'm intervening. You're off track, and you need help."

"Then the word isn't in this place?"

"It *is* in this place."

"Then how can I be off track?"

"It *is* here, but you didn't have to come here to find it. In fact, you didn't even have to leave your home."

"But if it's here, I don't understand how I can be off track or why you would have to come to intervene."

"I came to help you find the Third Harbinger and to give you the key to unlock *all* the Harbingers."

"I'm listening."

"The Nine Harbingers, what are they?" he asked.

"Signs…warnings…given to a nation in danger of judgment."

"And to whom did they first appear?"

"To the people of ancient Israel."

"And when did they first appear?"

"At the time of the breach, the first invasion."

"So then that's where you need to look, Nouriel. In 732 B.C. when the Assyrians invaded the land, that's where the word is."

"What does that mean?"

"A word was given, a prophetic word."

"The word I've been searching for?"

"Yes."

With that, he reached into the inner lining of his coat and pulled out an object…a roll. He placed it on the table and carefully began unrolling it under the incandescent glow of the lamp. It appeared to be an ancient parchment on which were written words of an ancient-looking script.

"It looks like a piece of the Dead Sea Scrolls," I said. It was the nearest thing I could think of to describe what I was seeing.

"It does," he replied.

"But it's not a piece of the Dead Sea Scrolls."

"No, but close."

"What is it?"

He didn't answer. But, passing his finger over the parchment, he began reading aloud the ancient words. *"Davar, Shalakh, Adonai."*

"Which means what?" I asked.

"Davar…a word; *Shalakh*…has been sent."

"'A word has been sent,'" I repeated.

"Adonai…the Lord."

"'A word has been sent…Lord?'"

"A word has been sent *by* the Lord," he said, correcting my translation. *"Davar, Shalakh, Adonai.* The Lord has sent a word. *B'Yaakov*…to Jacob; and it has fallen upon Israel, and all the people will know it. Ephraim, and those who dwell in Samaria who, in pride and arrogance of heart, say…"

"Say…what?"

"What I'm about to read, Nouriel, is the message given to ancient Israel in the days after that first attack. In this lies the key to unlock all the Harbingers."

"How?"

"By revealing their mysteries—the key to the nation's future."

"The future of ancient Israel."

"And the future of America."

Once again he began passing his finger over the scroll and reciting its ancient words: "This is the message," said the prophet. "Listen carefully:

- "*L'vanaim*—The bricks

- "*Nafaloo*—Have fallen

- "*V'Gazit*—But with hewn stone

- "*Nivneh*—We will rebuild

- "*Shikmim*—The sycamores

- "*Gooda'oo*—Have been cut down

- "*V'Erazim*—But with cedars

- "*NaKhalif*—We will plant in their place

> "The bricks have fallen,
> But we will rebuild with hewn stone;
> The sycamores have been cut down,
> But we will plant cedars in their place."[1]

———————————◆◆◆———————————

"It wasn't what I expected him to say," Nouriel said.

"What did you expect?" she asked.

"Something relevant, something of significance. What did bricks and sycamore trees have to do with America—or anything? And I told him."

———————————◆◆◆———————————

"I don't understand," I said. "I don't even know what it's saying. How is it the key?"

"This is Israel's response to that first invasion, the first calamity. These are the words that sum up the nation's spirit—a spirit of pride, defiance, and arrogance in the face of the calamity."

"And why is it significant?" I asked.

"Because these are the words that seal the nation's course and foretell its future."

"I'm not seeing it."

"What exactly is it, Nouriel, that they're really saying?"

"In the aftermath of the invasion they're going to rebuild."

"And why would that be significant?"

"I have no idea. It's what you do when something's destroyed—you rebuild."

"Look deeper, Nouriel. What's the larger context? A nation is turning away from God. Its hedge of protection has been removed. Why?"

"To cause them to turn back, to wake them up, to save them from a greater judgment."

"And what are they doing in light of it? Or rather, what are they *not* doing?"

"They're not returning to God?"

"Exactly. Instead of listening to the alarm, instead of turning back, instead of even pausing for a moment to reexamine their ways, they boast of their resolve. It wasn't about rebuilding at all. It was about ignoring the warning and rejecting the call to return."

"So they missed their warning."

"They did more than just miss it. They defied it. Notice the words. They weren't vowing just to rebuild what was destroyed, but to make themselves stronger than before, to become invulnerable to any future attack. So what they're saying is this: 'We will not be humbled. We will not search our ways or consider the possibility that something could be wrong. Instead, we'll defy the calamity. We'll beat it back. We'll rebuild. We'll undo the damage as if it never happened. Not only will we not change our course—we'll pursue it now with even more zeal. We'll come out of this calamity stronger than ever and rise to even greater heights than before.'"

"They were saying all that in those few words?" I asked.

"That's exactly what they were saying. That's exactly what it means. The alarm had sounded, and they were vowing to silence it. And what happens, Nouriel, if you silence an alarm?"

"You keep sleeping."

"And if the alarm was to warn you of a danger...what then?"

"Then the danger becomes even more dangerous...because now you have nothing to warn you that it's coming."

"Exactly. So they kept sleeping. They nullified the alarm that was meant to wake them up...to save them. And it was all there in the vow:

"The bricks have fallen,
But we will rebuild with hewn stone;
The sycamores have been cut down,
But we will plant cedars in their place.

"These are the words that seal a nation's destiny."

"The fate of an entire nation hanging on so few words?"

"And in the original language, even fewer...eight words."

"But how?" I asked.

"The vow was a sign, a manifestation of the hardening of their hearts, the rejection of God's calling, the sealing of the nation's defiance and its course—and thus the sealing of its end. So the vow itself is a sign of judgment."

"Question...You told me that the word I was looking for wasn't just here in this library, that I didn't have to come here to find it. How could I possibly have found that parchment without you showing it to me?"

"It's not the parchment," he answered, "It's the word. And the word is from a book, from the book of a prophet..."

"A prophet?"

"...who lived at the time of the invasion...and through whom the word was given."

"And the prophet was...?"

"*Yishaiyahu.*"

"I've never heard of him."

"You have, you just didn't know his real name. You know him as *Isaiah.*"

"Isaiah."

"The word is from the Bible...from the Book of Isaiah...the ninth chapter...Isaiah 9:10."

"Isaiah 9:10. So it's known."

"Not really. It's a very obscure verse. Even most of those who read the Bible every day would have little idea it even existed."

"So what does all this have to do with America?"

"The prophecy, in its context, concerned ancient Israel. But now, as a *sign*, it concerns America."

"How?"

"It's the sign of a nation that once knew God but then fell away, a sign that America is now the nation in danger of judgment...and now given warning and the call to return."

"So it was originally given to Israel, but now it's given as a *sign* to America?"

"Yes. So if that same prophetic message, that same warning of judgment, once given in Israel's last days, should now manifest itself in America, it will be a sign—a sign that *America* is now the nation that once knew God but then fell away and is now in danger of judgment and now given warning and a calling to return."

"So if that word should be manifested in America, it becomes a harbinger of America's future?"

"A harbinger," he answered, "and more than one."

"The Nine Harbingers."

"Yes. The Nine Harbingers—each one joined to the ancient prophecy, each one joined to this word, and each one carrying a revelation. If these harbingers of Israel's judgment should now reappear, along with this prophetic word, then the nation in which they reappear is in danger."

"And you're saying that they *have* reappeared."

"Yes."

"All of them?"

"All nine."

"And they've all reappeared in America?"

"Yes."

"And they all concern America?"

"Yes."

"And Isaiah 9:10 is the key to all of them?"

"Yes. It's the key that unlocks each of their mysteries and joins them all together. Each of the Harbingers is connected. Each, when joined together with the other eight, forms a prophetic message. Each mystery is itself a puzzle piece in a still larger mystery."

"So two of the Harbingers you've revealed. What are the other seven?"

"Ah," he replied, "that would be telling. It's for you to find them."

"And it's for you to help me."

"I have. I just gave you the key."

"You could give me a little more to go on."

He paused, as if carefully pondering every word that was about to proceed out of his mouth. Then just as carefully and deliberately he began to speak.

"Two of the nine you already know, the Breach and the Terrorist. These form the context. As for the other seven, one is of stone; the other is fallen. One ascends. One is alive; the other once was. One speaks of what is; and the other speaks of what would be."

There was a long pause before I ventured a response.

"You know," I said, "I'm not telling you how to do your job, but this would all be a lot easier if you just gave me a map and a few subway tokens."

"You don't need a token; you have the key."

"And what do I do with it?"

"You use it to find the Third Harbinger."

Chapter 7

The Third Harbinger:
The Fallen Bricks

ח א

WE GOT UP from the table, left the reading room, and made our way down and out the library's front entrance.

"So this time he didn't vanish at the end of the encounter," Ana observed.

"No. Either that or it wasn't the end of the encounter. We started down the front steps. That's when it hit me. We were standing right under one of the lions when I realized it. That's where I stopped to take out the seal and look at it once more."

◆◆◆

"I have it!" I said.

"You have what?" he asked.

"The Third Harbinger. I know what it is."

"And what is it?"

"It's the bricks from the prophecy...from Isaiah: '*The bricks have fallen.*' That's how it begins...the image on the seal. That's what is in ruins...fallen bricks...a pile of fallen bricks."

"Very good, Nouriel. Now tell me what it means."

"It would be the ruins left in the wake of the Assyrian invasion."

"Correct. When the Assyrian attack was over, the people of Israel began surveying the damage. What they found were the ruins of collapsed buildings, heaps of rubble and fallen brick. *The bricks had fallen.* They were fragile to begin with, bricks of clay and straw and dried in the midday sun. Any building made of these would be especially vulnerable to destruction. So the pile of fallen brick became the most visible sign of the calamity and of the fact that the nation's existence now rested on shaky ground. It was now vulnerable and in danger. The breach had been made, and the destruction, though limited, had begun."

"So the ruin heap of fallen bricks was a sign," I said, "not just of what *had* happened, but of what *would* happen if the nation didn't change its course."

"Exactly...the sign of collapse, the collapse of a building, the collapse of a kingdom, and then of a civilization."

He asked me for the seal, and then, lifting it up, he began to explain its meaning. "The Third Harbinger: Enemies enter the land and cause destruction. The destruction leaves the nation traumatized. But the scope and duration of that destruction are limited. The most visible signs of the attack is the ruin heaps of fallen bricks, stone, and rubble where once had stood a building. 'The bricks have fallen.' The Third Harbinger: the Fallen Bricks."

"Ground Zero."

"As the dust of September 11 settled on New York City, people emerged to survey the damage. The World Trade Center had collapsed into a colossal heap of ruins. As Americans watched on their television sets and computer screens, the image of the colossal ruin heap at Ground Zero became the most visible and identifiable sign of what had happened...a strange image, several stories high, surreal, and haunting. In the days and weeks that followed, the image would be seared into the nation's collective consciousness—a sign of destruction, though, as with ancient Israel, a destruction limited in scope and duration. And yet, as in the ancient case, the ruin heap would serve as a sign against the nation's sense of invulnerability. America was now vulnerable. The breach had been made. The stones were coming undone. And the nation's security was resting on shaky ground."

"But the World Trade Center wasn't made out of clay bricks," I countered.

"The effect, though, was the same. The ancient prophecy opens up with the image of collapse—the ruins of fallen buildings. It was the same image of collapse and of the ruins of fallen buildings that confronted America in those first dark days following September 11. The American towers fell with the same suddenness as did the clay bricks and buildings of ancient Israel. In a matter of moments, they had become a heap of ruins. And yet the connection was still more literal."

"What do you mean?"

"The ruin heap of Ground Zero was filled with steel, concrete, and glass, but not only that."

"With what?"

"Bricks."

"As in 'The bricks have fallen.'"

"The fallen bricks of ancient Israel comprised a warning concerning the nation's future. So too the fallen bricks of Ground Zero. The World Trade Center was a symbol of America's economic power—proud, majestic, towering. But in a matter of moments it had come crashing down to dust...a warning to even the most proud, majestic, and towering of nations that no nation is invulnerable or exempt from the day that its power comes crashing down to earth, even in a moment's time."

"'The bricks have fallen'; it's not just about destruction. It's about a nation's response to destruction, its vow of defiance. So how did America's reaction to 9/11 compare to that of ancient Israel?"

"Do you remember the days that followed 9/11?" he asked.

"Of course," I answered.

"No one had to say it. It was as if almost everyone had some sort of sense about it, even if they couldn't put it into words. It was as if the nation had unconsciously heard a silent voice calling it to be still and to return to the foundation."

"The voice of God?"

"Yes, and for a moment, America appeared to be responding. The rush and clamor of its culture were stilled. Wall Street came to a standstill. Hollywood grew silent. Throughout the nation there was a noticeable and massive turning away from the superficial and to the spiritual. Even the name of God was taken out of the closet and publicly proclaimed from Capitol Hill to New York City. Multitudes sang "God Bless America" and gathered for prayer. America's houses of worship overflowed with throngs of people seeking to find solace. In those first few days and weeks after 9/11, it seemed as if there might be a true national turning, a changing of course, an awakening—even a spiritual revival."

"But then America *was* turning back to God?"

"No. America was not turning back to God. It was a spiritual revival that never came. And even the appearance of turning back was short-lived. It had no real root. There was no real change of heart or course, no searching of ways, no questioning if something could be wrong, no repentance. So it couldn't last. And it wasn't long before the moment was lost and things began to return to a form of normalcy. The calls for prayer would fade away, the rush and clamor of daily life would resume, the spiritual searching would be abandoned, and the superficial again embraced. The name of God would again be withdrawn from the public square, and most of those who had suddenly flocked to houses of worship would cease their flocking. The nation would resume its departure from God and its rejection of His ways, only now with increased speed."

"So how did America's response to 9/11 compare with Israel's response in Isaiah 9:10?"

"It was the same. From one commentary…"

"Commentary?"

"The commentaries are writings on the Bible explaining the meaning, verse by verse."

"But not *the* Bible."

"Not the Word of God, but commentary on the Word of God."

"So you study the commentaries?" I asked, surprised at the idea of it.

"I have."

"I just didn't picture a prophet studying the…"

"And why not?" he replied. "Is God not able to speak through such things?"

"I guess He is…"

"One commentary on Isaiah 9:10 describes how the people of ancient Israel viewed their national calamity:

"There is no way for the people to ignore the obvious disaster. Yet they choose not to recognize its deeper meaning...they do not respond to God. They only respond (inadequately) to the threatening situation.[1]

"Take those same words and bring them into the twenty-first century, and you have a description of post-9/11 America."

"So then it would mean that in the wake of 9/11, America only responded to the immediate and obvious situation, to the destruction caused by the calamity and to the danger it threatened...but never considered that there could be anything deeper...no significance behind the obvious."

"'The bricks have fallen...*but*...' That was the point. Another commentary on the ancient vow puts it this way:

"The people, declared the prophet, did not take this calamity as a judgment from God but hardened their hearts and declared: 'The bricks are fallen, but we will build with hewn stone; the sycamores are cut down, but we will put cedars in their place.'"[2]

"Then America was shutting off the alarm..."

"Yes...silencing the alarm meant to awaken it."

"Did anyone realize it?"

"Some...while others sensed something more...something deeper...but couldn't put their finger on exactly what it was. But the alarm had sounded. The nation was in danger. Its bricks had fallen. Its stones were loosening. And it was only the beginning. *The bricks have fallen* is only the opening of the ancient vow. There was more of the mystery to unfold. It's what happened *after* 9/11 that would prove even more ominous."

———— ◆◆◆ ————

It was then that he opened his right hand, exposing the next seal. "The seal of the Fourth Harbinger," he said as he handed it to me. "This one, Nouriel, is different."

"The seal?"

"No," he answered, "the Harbinger. Unlike the first three, the Fourth Harbinger was conceived on American soil, and it wasn't set in motion by the nation's enemies."

"Then who set it in motion?"

"American leaders."

"American leaders?"

"Yes."

"And how will I know it?"

"It's hard to miss. It's the largest one."

Chapter 8

The Fourth Harbinger: The Tower

אָ ת

"CAN I GET you something else?" she asked. "Something other than water?"

"No, I'm fine," he replied.

"I apologize. I should have asked you when you first came."

"The water's fine," he replied.

"So," she said, changing her pace and tone, "he gave you the seal of the Fourth Harbinger. And what was on it?"

"Images and markings, just like the others. But its central image looked something like the Tower of Babel."

"And how would you know what the Tower of Babel looked like?" she asked with a trace of friendly skepticism in her voice.

"I don't," he replied, "but I've seen pictures of it. The image looked like a *ziggurat*...a terraced tower with each terrace or story getting smaller and smaller as it rises."

"And what did you make of it?"

"I didn't know what to make of it. I looked up everything I could on the Tower of Babel. But there was nothing I could find to connect to the seal. So I went back to the vow in Isaiah 9:10. But there was no mention of a tower. I was going nowhere."

"As you were before."

"As I was before except then I didn't realize I was going nowhere. This time I was going nowhere and knowing I was going nowhere. I guess it was some sort of improvement, but it's easier to go nowhere when you don't realize that's where you're going."

"So what did you do?"

"I put the two clues together—the image on the seal with what he told me."

"What he told you...was what?"

"When I asked him how I would know the Fourth Harbinger, he told me it would be hard to miss—it was the largest one. So there's the image of a tower and the clue that the Fourth Harbinger is the largest one, the largest *tower*. So I went to the largest standing tower in New York City."

"The Empire State Building?"

"Yes. To the eighty-sixth floor and outside to the observation deck. It was early evening...a windy day...just around sunset...with thousands of lights just beginning to appear throughout the cityscape. I walked around the deck gazing at the skyscrapers in every direction, but there was nothing that struck me as being especially significant with regard to the clues. I was standing on the south side looking out to the city's lower end. To my left was a man viewing the same scene through one of the metal telescopes they have there, the ones you have to pay to look through, the ones with timers on them."

———— ◆◆◆ ————

"Impressive," the man said. "It's an impressive view."

"Yes it is," I answered."

"So many towers."

———— ◆◆◆ ————

"When I heard the word *towers*, I turned around. It was *him*."

"The prophet, looking through a telescope on the observation deck of the Empire State Building?"

"The same."

"And you didn't notice him before that?"

"I was looking at the view, not the people. And his face was hidden behind the telescope."

"But his voice."

"Yes, but out of context, I wasn't expecting to hear it."

———— ◆◆◆ ————

The prophet continued. "It has a beauty to it," he said, still gazing at the scenery, "a strange beauty."

"Don't tell me you just came up here to take in the view," I said.

"Actually, I had an appointment," he replied.

"There's no point in me asking you how you do all this, is there?" I asked. "My guess is that it involves satellites." I was being facetious of course.

"You're right," he said.

"That it involves satellites?"

"No," he replied, "that there's no point in asking."

"How long have you been here?"

"Long enough," he answered. "I was wondering when you'd get here."

"The clue on the seal, it's a tower, right?"

"It *is* a tower."

"Then I have it right this time. It's the Empire State Building."

"No," he replied. "You've gotten it wrong again."

"What do you mean? It's a tower…the largest tower…and you're here."

"The image on the seal is a tower. But the Empire State Building is just the place of our meeting."

"But you said it was the largest one."

"The largest of the *Harbingers.*"

"Then the Fourth Harbinger *isn't* a tower?"

"I didn't say that. But it isn't *this* tower. How many towers do you see out there?"

"I have no idea."

"Many. And to which one do you think the seal points?" Just then he looked up from the telescope. His time was up. He turned to me.

"Do you need some change?" I asked, half-facetiously.

"I'm OK," he answered. He began walking along the deck. I walked alongside him. He turned again to take in the view. I did likewise. So we both stood there in the wind, looking out at the vast expanse of skyscrapers, more and more of them now dotted with yellow lights and set against the deep red and blue background of the sunset sky.

"And where were you now on the deck?" she asked.

"Still on the south side, facing lower Manhattan."

"Nouriel," he asked, "where are we in the prophecy, in Isaiah 9:10?"

"*The bricks have fallen,*" I replied.

"That revealed the First Harbinger. But where are we now? What comes next?"

"*The bricks have fallen,*' but..."

"*But we will rebuild,*'" he said, completing the sentence. "That's the key to the Fourth Harbinger."

"It doesn't sound very revealing."

"Remember, it's not just the words but the context surrounding them and the spirit behind them. The problem wasn't the rebuilding. The problem was the spirit and the motive behind the rebuilding. They had just been given a critical warning. But they respond with defiance: '*But we will rebuild*' is the first declaration of that defiance, from which will come their judgment."

"It doesn't only say, '*We will rebuild,*' I added. "It says, '*We will rebuild with hewn stone.*' Hewn stone...what's that about? What's the significance?"

"The fallen bricks were made of clay and straw. They were brittle and flimsy. They would be replaced, but not with more clay bricks, but with something much stronger—hewn stone."

"So a building made of stone would be much more resistant to any future attack."

"Exactly, and it could rise to greater heights."

"So the hewn stone signifies their intent to come out of the attack stronger than they were before it."

"Yes...again...all about defiance. Instead of being humbled by the calamity, they become emboldened by it. They vow to build bigger, better, stronger, and higher than before. Not only will they continue on their course of apostasy—now they'll do it with a vengeance, with defiance. So instead of bowing their heads before heaven, they raise their fists against it."

"So what happened?" I asked

"They clear away the heaps of fallen brick and rubble and begin the reconstruction on the ground of their devastation. The project is filled with symbolic meaning. It represents the nation's rebuilding of itself and its rise from the ashes. The vow would become reality. New buildings, stronger, taller, bigger, and better, would rise up in place of those destroyed in the attack. So the new construction would become a concrete manifestation and witness of the nation's defiance of God's call."

Taking the seal in his right hand and lifting it up, he began to explain. "The Fourth Harbinger: In the wake of the calamity, the nation responds without repentance, humility, or reflection, but with pride and defiance. Their leaders vow, '*We will rebuild.*' They pledge to rebuild bigger, better, taller, and stronger than before. The rebuilding takes place on the ground of destruction. The construction is intended to be a symbol of national resurgence. It is set to rise up from the ruins of that which had fallen and to surpass it in height. It will be their towering testament of defiance—the rebuilding of the fallen, and of the nation itself, the Fourth Harbinger...the Tower."

"So if the ancient mystery is joined to America, then somehow 9/11 has to be linked to the words '*We will rebuild.*'"

"Correct. In the wake of their calamity, the leaders of ancient Israel proclaimed, '*We will rebuild*'—the first sign of defiance. If the mystery holds and has now applied to America, we would expect to hear the same vow, the same three words, in the wake of 9/11, now proclaimed by American leaders."

"And did it happen? Did they say it?"

"Yes. They said it. Not that it wouldn't have been natural to speak of rebuilding, but the way these three words continuously came forth from the mouths of American leaders, spoken, over and over again, as public proclamations, was striking.

"From the mayor of New York City in the wake of the attack: '*We will rebuild...*'[1]

"From the state's senior senator: '*We will rebuild...*'[2]

"From the state's governor: '*We will rebuild. And we will move forward.*'[3]

"From the state's junior senator: '*We will rebuild...*'[4]

"From the city's mayor at the time of the rebuilding: '*We will rebuild, renew, and remain the capital of the free world.*'[5]

"From the president of the United States: '*We will rebuild New York City.*'[6]

"One way or another, each leader would end up proclaiming the same words of defiance proclaimed thousands of years before by the leaders of ancient Israel."

"And as with ancient Israel, it wasn't just the speaking of words."

"That's correct, Nouriel. The words were followed by action."

"So what happened after the words were spoken by the American leaders?"

"The words were likewise followed by action. The ruins of 9/11 were cleared away. Then a sign appeared at Ground Zero with these words: '*A new icon will soon rise above the Lower Manhattan skyline...the Freedom Tower.*'[7]

"The Tower!"

"Exactly. It would become the center point of the rebuilding."

"And the sign called it *an icon*. It was meant to be a symbol of the rebuilding, of Ground Zero and the nation."

"It was to be an icon of defiance. *Defiance*—the word comes up again and again in the commentaries. Listen:

> "It is *the defiance* of a people who, far from being repentant, glory in their iniquity.[8]

> "To be heedless when God is speaking, by whatever voice He may address us, is surely iniquitous enough, but to act in *deliberate defiance of the Almighty* is, by many degrees, worse.[9]

> "Proud *defiance* of God always brings disaster.[10]

"Long before the rebuilding began, while the dust of the attack still hovered above the ground of devastation, an American senator would foretell the meaning of the future campaign:

> "I believe one of the first things we should commit to—with federal help that underscores our nation's purpose—*is to rebuild* the towers of the World Trade Center and show the world we are not afraid—*WE ARE DEFIANT*."[11]

"Is it about the leaders then?" I asked.

"No," said the prophet, "not specifically."

"Then about those making the proclamations?"

"No," he repeated. "These are prophetic reenactments or prophetic manifestations, the first of many. And though they involve people, they're not about the people involved. Those involved act unwittingly, without realizing what they're doing, as representatives of the nation, agents of a national spirit. These are prophetic signs *of* and *to* a nation. So the campaign to rebuild was not about any one person or any group of people. It was the will of a nation, the manifestation of a national spirit. One journalist would describe it this way: 'Rebuilding Ground Zero was going to be *America's statement of defiance* to those who attacked us.'"[12]

"*A statement of defiance*, exactly what the ancient vow was...a statement of defiance."

"Of defiance and boasting. From the commentaries:

> "They rise upon the ruins of their broken homes...boasting that they will *show the enemy, whether God or man*, that they can 'take it.'[13]

"Two and half thousand years later, the governor of New York would proclaim the same thing from the pavement of Ground Zero: 'Let this great Freedom Tower *show the world that what our enemies sought to destroy...stands taller than ever.*'[14]

"From the words of the commentaries on Isaiah 9:10:

"They boasted that they would rebuild their devastated country and *make it stronger and more glorious than ever before.*[15]

"From the words of the mayor of New York in response to 9/11: 'We will rebuild. We're going to come out of this stronger than before, politically stronger, economically stronger.'"[16]

◆◆◆

"These were all verbatim," asked Ana, "actual quotes?"

"Yes."

"And what did you think when you heard them?"

"It was eerie. Modern American leaders voicing the same things voiced in ancient Israel, and words that had to do with judgment. It was eerie."

"And what else did he tell you?"

"He spoke of the difference between *restoration* and *defiance*."

"Which is...?"

◆◆◆

"To replace bricks with bricks is restoration," he said. "But to replace bricks with hewn stone is defiance. To rebuild what was destroyed is restoration, but to boast of rebuilding stronger and greater than before is defiance. The Fourth Harbinger is not simply about rebuilding what was destroyed, but it must specifically involve rebuilding bigger, taller, stronger, and better than before. That distinction is clear in the Scripture and in the commentaries:

> "Since their houses had been destroyed, *they would build bigger, better, and finer ones.*[17]

"So too it came out in the words of those attempting to rebuild Ground Zero. One of the nation's most prominent real estate magnates said this of the proposed project:

> "...we should have the World Trade Center *bigger and better.*[18]

"From the commentaries on ancient Israel:

"If they ruin our houses, we will repair them, and make them stronger and finer than they were before.[19]

"From the American magnate, on the rebuilding of Ground Zero:

"What I want to see built is the World Trade Center *stronger and maybe a story taller.*[20]

"You see, Nouriel, even if by just as little as one story, it was not about rebuilding—it was about defiance, just as it was in ancient Israel. From the commentaries on the meaning behind Israel's rebuilding:

"They are determined to withstand God and rebuild on an even grander scale.[21]

"Now, in the words of one observer, the meaning behind the rebuilding of Ground Zero:

"The developer who holds the lease *has vowed that the towers will rise again*...it would show us *defiant in the face of terror, unbowed, climbing again gleaming into the sky taller, bigger, stronger.*[22]

"Notice the wording: *unbowed, climbing into the sky, taller, bigger, stronger...defiant.* In other words, the rebuilding of Ground Zero, the Tower, would be the embodiment of a defiant nation, just as in Isaiah 9:10."

"He even used the word *vowed.*"

"Correct. It was a vow, and a boast. In fact, for a time, they even boasted that the Tower of Ground Zero would overshadow every other building on earth; Isaiah 9:10 to the extreme."

"And what happened to that boast?"

"It would ultimately be thwarted. But that's how it began. The rebuilding of Ground Zero was supposed to have resulted in the tallest building in the world."

"A question," I said. "I understand the Tower as a symbol of the reconstruction, but is there any place in Isaiah that actually speaks of a tower?"

"Centuries before the writing of the New Testament, the Hebrew Scriptures were translated into Greek. The result was a Greek version of the Hebrew Scriptures called the *Septuagint*. The Septuagint version of Isaiah 9:10 renders the rebuilding project in even more specific terms. It says this:

> "The bricks are fallen down...*but come...let us build for ourselves a TOWER.*"[23]

"How does this happen?" I asked. "How does it all come together, the words of the leaders, the vows, the Tower? It's amazing, as if it's all part of some kind of reenactment."

"The reenactment of an ancient drama of judgment," he answered. "A reenactment in which none of the players have any idea they're doing it." With that he became silent, and we both gazed out into the vast expanse that surrounded us, now darker and more aglow with lights.

"And so," he said, breaking the silence, "out of the ruins of the nation's calamity emerges the Fourth Harbinger, the most colossal of Harbingers, a Tower—and the most soaring testament of defiance ever to stand on American soil."

◆◆◆

And again he became silent and just stood there on the deck in the wind, looking out into the lights and darkness of the cityscape.

"A strange beauty when you look at it from here," he remarked softly. Then he opened his hand. "The seal of the Fifth Harbinger."

I took it, examined it, then placed it in my pocket. "What can you tell me about it?" I asked.

"It's a Harbinger of foundations."

"Where do I find it?"

"Away from here."

"You're sure you're not giving away too much information?"

"*Far* away from here."

Chapter 9

The Fifth Harbinger: The Gazit Stone

א ח

"SO WHAT WAS on the seal?" she asked.

"An irregular line...ascending and descending. I took it to be the top of a mountain."

"And where did that lead you?"

"I looked at Isaiah 9, but there was nothing there about a mountain. I couldn't find anything to connect the seal to the prophecy, much less to 9/11. Again I found myself at a roadblock...going nowhere...until I went deeper."

"Deeper?"

"Into the prophecy. The last Harbinger focused on the word *rebuild*."

"But we will rebuild."

"Yes, *We will rebuild*, but with what? I focused on the next word."

"But we will rebuild *with hewn stone*."

"But I thought that was part of the mystery of the Tower...that they would replace what was destroyed with something greater and stronger than before."

"It *was*. But the prophecy specifically speaks about a stone."

"A hewn stone."

"Yes, but it was originally written in Hebrew. That's where I went deeper. I looked up the Hebrew behind the word *stone*."

"And..."

"The word is *gazit*. It could be called the *Gazit Stone*. It can be translated as, *a hewn stone, a carved stone, a dressed stone, a smooth stone, a cut stone*, or *a quarried stone*. The Gazit Stone was, most specifically, a stone quarried, chiseled, and carved out of mountain rock."

"*Mountain* rock!" she said as if proud to have come up with the discovery. "There's your connection!"

"Exactly. And after being quarried, it would be leveled, smoothed, and shaped into a block for use in building, a building block. After the Assyrian attack, the people of Israel would set out to rebuild. They would go to the mountains and quarries to carve, shape, and smooth the Gazit Stone. Then they would bring it back to where the bricks had fallen so the rebuilding could begin."

"So you actually put the clues together correctly."

"I believe it was the first time I did—a major accomplishment."

"Where did it lead you?"

"Nowhere. It led me nowhere. I was able to connect the stone to the mountain, but nothing else. There was nothing connecting it to now...no connection to America. How many new buildings in this city do they build out of mountain stone? There was no link."

"So what did you do?"

"I took a break. I took a break from trying to figure it out...and from the city. I went upstate; there's a cabin there by a lake that I rent. I had several projects to work on. So I got away."

"So you put the search behind you."

"The search, yes, but not the seal. I didn't want to leave that behind."

"So what happened?"

"For the first two days...nothing. It was uneventful. Then, on the third day, I was out driving, to nowhere in particular, just a drive in the countryside. That's when I saw it...on my left...in the distance."

"That's when you saw *what*?"

"A mountain."

"There had to be a lot of mountains upstate."

"But this one looked familiar. I pulled over and got out of the car. I reached into my pocket to look at the seal. And it matched."

"The mountain matched the image on the seal?" she said, with obvious disbelief.

"It was the same shape, the same outline, the same mountain."

"But I thought the seal was ancient, from the Middle East. How could it match a mountain in America?"

"I don't know. Maybe it was the image of another mountain, some mountain in the Middle East that happened to match the mountain I saw that day. I don't know...but it matched."

"But for that to happen, the image would not only have had to match the mountain but the view from which you saw the mountain. How could that happen?"

"How could any of it happen?" he said, as if expecting her to by now take such things for granted. "How could I keep meeting him each time? Some kind of destiny...or predestination...something. Anyway, it matched, or it appeared to match, the moment I first saw it, and from the very spot from which I saw it."

"So you pursued it."

"Of course. I drove up the mountain as far as I could drive then went on foot the rest of the way."

"And what did you find?"

"I figured that whatever I was supposed to find would be on the mountaintop. But the mountain was long and rolling and was covered with trees. It was hard to know where to look, not to mention what exactly I was looking for. I was there for hours, from midday to the late afternoon. And then, in the late afternoon, I finally found what I was supposed to find."

"Which was?"

"*Him*. I found *him*. The first thing I noticed was the coat...that long dark coat flapping with each gust of wind. He was standing there by one of the edges of the mountaintop, looking out into the distance."

"He was often doing that...looking out into the distance...right?"

"Yes. And now it was into a vast open landscape of distant blue mountains, all different shades of blue blending into each other, something you'd see in a watercolor."

"And he just *happened* to be there when you *happened* to be there. And you just *happened* to be there only because you just *happened* to be driving by that particular place that day, and you just *happened* to see the mountain from a view that just *happened* to match the image of the mountain on the seal." She paused and stared at him with a light smile before adding, "It all just *happened* to *happen*."

"That's pretty much it," he replied

"And how far away was the mountain from the city?"

"Several hours north."

"How did he…?"

"Don't even try. So I approached him. I was within ten feet of him when he spoke."

◆◆◆

"So how was your vacation, Nouriel?" he asked, without looking back.

"You know, I promised myself I wasn't going to ask how you do all this…but how long have you been here…on this mountain…on this spot?"

"Not long…just enough to be here before you came. I didn't want to keep you waiting. That wouldn't be polite."

"But of course."

"So you had a pleasant vacation?"

"I'm still in the midst of it, and I'm not sure." I was now standing at his side near the edge, facing him. He would alternate his gaze between me and the light blue mountains in the distance.

"So what have you found so far?" he asked.

"On the Fifth Harbinger? Not a lot."

"Then let's start with the little…what have you found?"

"After the attack, the nation vows to rebuild, not with clay bricks, as before, but with stone. In the prophecy, the Hebrew word for stone is *gazit*."

"Well done, Nouriel. You're going deeper. That's good. What else?"

"*Gazit* speaks of stone that's been cut out, chiseled, in particular, quarried from mountain rock. Thus the mountain on the seal…a place from which the gazit stone is quarried."

"That's more than a little."

"But it doesn't lead me anywhere."

"It led you here."

"But what does it have to do with America…or with the Tower? It's not as if New York City is about to build skyscrapers out of quarried stones."

"Piece the clues together, Nouriel. Then we can see if there's any connection to America. Where are we in the prophecy?"

"But we will rebuild with hewn stone."

"So they vow to rebuild and to do so stronger than before…to replace the fallen clay bricks with the gazit stone. They quarry their stones, carve them into massive blocks, and bring them back to the ground of destruction, to where the bricks have fallen. The first stone of building is always the most important—the cornerstone. The laying down of the cornerstone begins the construction. It's not just a necessary act, but a symbolic one. And in the case of Israel's rebuilding, the laying down of the first gazit stone would be filled with symbolic meaning, signaling the beginning of the nation's rebuilding and the fulfillment of its vow. May I have the seal?"

So I handed it to him, and he lifted it up as he revealed its meaning. "The Fifth Harbinger: The nation responds to the calamity with defiance in the form of stone. The stone is cut out of their mountains and bedrock. They chisel it into a block. They bring it back to the ground of destruction. The stone becomes a symbol, the embodiment of their vow, their confidence, and their defiance. Upon the stone they rest their plans of rebuilding and their vow of national resurgence. But the Gazit Stone is, in reality, a symbol of a nation's rejection of God's calling. When the sign of the Gazit Stone manifests, it's a Harbinger carrying a warning of future calamity. The Fifth Harbinger: the Gazit Stone."

"And what does it have to do with America?"

"They came here, Nouriel. They came here to find the Gazit Stone."

"Here?" I asked.

"Here…to the mountains. They came here and cut it out of the mountain rock and brought it back."

"Back?"

"Back to where the bricks had fallen."

"To Ground Zero?"

"Yes. For the vow declares, '*The bricks have fallen, but we will rebuild with quarried stone.*' So the rebuilding must begin on the same site of the destruction. So the Gazit Stone must be brought to where the bricks had fallen, to the ground of the calamity. Thus, the quarried stone had to be brought back to Ground Zero. And so it was."

"And what happened at Ground Zero once they brought it back?"

"There was a gathering there, a gathering of leaders—the mayor of New York City, the governor of New York State, the governor of New Jersey, various officials involved with the rebuilding, other leaders, and a gathering of guests and spectators. They were all focused on a single object—the Gazit Stone. The Gazit Stone most often took the form of a massive rectangular block of cut rock, so too the stone that was laid on the pavement of Ground Zero."

"A massive rectangular block of quarried stone...laid at Ground Zero?"

"A twenty-ton massive rectangular block of quarried stone. The stone was to mark the beginning of the rebuilding."

"*But we will rebuild with quarried stone.*"

"Exactly. The stone of Isaiah's prophecy was another symbol of national defiance. So too they made the Gazit Stone of Ground Zero into a symbol. They even gave it a name. They called it the *Freedom Stone*. It was created to be the symbolic cornerstone of the rebuilding—not just of Ground Zero, but of New York City and America. Its laying down was to be the first act in that rebuilding and the beginning of the Tower that was to rise up from the site. So, as in the last days of ancient Israel, the Gazit Stone would again become the symbol of a nation's rebuilding and restoration."

"Were there any such proclamations or vows spoken," I asked, "when the Gazit Stone was laid at Ground Zero?"

"Why do you ask that?"

"Because the stone in Isaiah 9:10 was linked to the proclaiming of the vow."

"There were. There were such proclamations. And as in the ancient case, their proclamations joined the nation's rebuilding to the quarried stone. Their words were, in effect, a modern paraphrase of the ancient vow. On Ground Zero the American leaders declared that they too would *rebuild with quarried stone*. The stone, they declared, would be the beginning of the nation's rebuilding. It would:

> "...forever remain a *symbolic cornerstone for the rebuilding of New York and the nation*.[1]

"As it was in ancient Israel, the act of rebuilding with quarried stone was intended to send a message. So the governor of New York would proclaim:

> "By laying this magnificent cornerstone of hope, we are sending a message to the people around the world."[2]

"A message of defiance."

"Yes, a message of defiance. On one hand, a defiance of the calamity; but on the other, beneath the surface, something much deeper...a much deeper defiance...just as it was with ancient Israel. One commentary explains it this way:

> "Far from being humbled and becoming repentant as a result of the chastening judgments of the Lord, they are resolutely determined to withstand God and rebuild on an even grander scale: *'The bricks have crumbled, but we will rebuild with stone cut out of the quarry...'*"[3]

"*Stone cut out of the quarry*—just as the rebuilding of Ground Zero and of America involved the stone cut of the quarry...here."

"Yes. And even the New York governor would allude to the *stone cut out of the quarry* as he spoke his proclamation over the stone:

"Today we take twenty tons of *Adirondack granite, the bedrock of our state,* and place it as the foundation, *the bedrock of a new symbol of American strength and confidence.*[4]

"As it was with ancient Israel, the quarried stone would become the embodiment of a nation's misplaced confidence in its own power to emerge stronger than before. And the act of laying down the quarried stone would be a manifestation of what the commentaries call the *spirit of defiance*:

> "The bricks may have fallen down; it was of no consequence— they would build *with hewn stone....* Thus they breathed the very *spirit of defiance.*[5]

> "The nation...determines to act in a *spirit of defiance*...it will turn its fallen bricks *into massive stones.*"[6]

"*The spirit of defiance*... Why is that significant?"

"On the day that America officially began its rebuilding by replacing the fallen bricks of 9/11 with the Gazit Stone, the governor of New York would make a proclamation from the floor of Ground Zero. Listen to the words:

> "Today, we, the heirs of that revolutionary *spirit of defiance, lay this cornerstone...*"[7]

"He used those exact words?"

"Those exact words."

"The same words...and the same act—the quarried stone and the spirit of defiance."

"Joined together."

"Unbelievable...the whole thing is so..."

"It is...but it happened. The ancient drama reenacted on Ground Zero."

"And what happened after," I asked, "after the stone was laid?"

"What happened after was especially striking. The rebuilding of Ground Zero had already become tangled in a continual stream of controversy, confusion, obstacles, dissension, and conflict. Even after the stone was set in place, the tower's construction would be challenged, halted, redrawn, renamed, and reversed. The plans to rebuild Ground Zero would be frustrated for years. Eventually they would remove the stone from Ground Zero altogether."

"Strange," I said. "They removed the cornerstone, and after all those words."

"Strange and not so strange. The plans of ancient Israel to defiantly rebuild itself would likewise be frustrated. It would ultimately lead the nation to the point of destruction. The laying down of the Gazit Stone was one more link in a chain of judgment. The commentary goes on to reveal what it all leads to:

> "It will turn its fallen bricks into massive stones that will not fail…it was to be followed with fearful penalty…to be pressed on every hand by its enemies…to be prepared for still impending miseries.[8]

> "The defiance of God shuts out immeasurable good."[9]

"It's a replaying…it's all replaying itself, the whole thing. It's so…uncanny. And they had no idea what they were doing."

"That they were reenacting the ancient prophecy? No. And yet they each ended up stepping into the ancient footsteps. It was a prophetic act, taking place according to the mystery."

"So what does it all portend for America's future?"

"If those who came to Ground Zero that day to issue their proclamations had realized what it all portended…they would have stayed home."

◆◆◆

He reached into his coat pocket and gave me the next seal.

"The seal of the Sixth Harbinger," I said. "And this is…?"

"The image is clear enough," he said, "as is the prophecy. This one shouldn't be hard to uncover."

"Still, some help would be appreciated."

"The Sixth Harbinger appeared the same day as the first…and in the same place of the one that came after it."

"Well, that really clears everything up," I replied. "And to think I was worried you wouldn't be specific enough this time."

"Nouriel."

"Yes?"

"Have a great rest of your vacation." And with that, he left me there…standing at the edge of the mountain.

"I'm sure I will," I answered in a raised voice.

"Try to get some rest," he responded as he walked. "Rest is good."

"And, of course, I'll be sure to bring you back a souvenir," I shouted.

"Just the seal, Nouriel. Just bring back the seal." And with that he disappeared into the woods.

Chapter 10

The Sixth Harbinger: The Sycamore

א ח

"H E SAID THE image was clear. So what was it?" she asked.
"A tree," he replied.

"A tree as in the prophecy?"

"Yes...as in the very next words of the prophecy."

"So the Harbingers were being revealed to you in the same order as they appeared in Isaiah 9:10."

"In the exact same order," he said. "The prophecy moves from the stone to the sycamore:

> "But we will rebuild with quarried stone. *The sycamores have been cut down.*"

"So the tree on the seal, it was a sycamore?" she asked.

"That's what I assumed."

"And so where did it lead you?"

"I went deeper, as before, into the original language to find the Hebrew behind the word *sycamore*."

"And you found..."

"*Shakam.* The word translated as *sycamore* is the Hebrew *shakam.* It's also known as the *fig mulberry* tree."

"How do you get sycamore from that?"

"The Greek word for *fig* is *sukos*, and for *mulberry* is *moros*. Put them together and you get *sukamoros* or..."

"Sycamore."

"Its Latin name is the *ficus sycamorus*...a wide-spreading tree that reaches a height of about fifty feet. In biblical times they grew in Israel's lowlands and along the roads and highways."

"So you did your homework."

"And I pursued it. I even took my quest to the New York Botanical Gardens...but it didn't lead me any closer to the mystery of the Sixth Harbinger. In fact, it led me farther away. The more I learned about the sycamore, the farther I was from the answer."

"Why?"

"What could the cutting down of a sycamore tree possibly have to do with America or 9/11? The ancient Assyrians may have been interested in cutting down sycamores, but not the terrorists of 9/11. They targeted cities, not forests or farmlands. How could the cutting down of a sycamore tree have anything to do with it? There was no connection. That was my first problem. But the second was fatal."

"Which was...?"

"It doesn't grow here, not in the American Northeast, not naturally. The ficus sycamorus is native to the Middle East and Africa. It doesn't grow in climates with frost. The only way you could keep it alive in New York or in Washington DC is to keep it inside or wrapped up in blankets and plastic. And some people actually do that. But it's a novelty. The sycamore of Isaiah 9:10 is alien to the American Northeast."

"So 9/11 had nothing to do with trees, and the sycamore has nothing to do with the Northeast. So what did you do?"

"After a few more dead-ends, I gave up trying. I figured that, somehow, whatever I was supposed to know, I would end up knowing."

"And did you end up knowing?"

"I ended up in Central Park, on the lake, in a rowboat. It's something I do when I need to clear my mind. There's a bridge there, a walking bridge, which stretches over the water in a long arch. If you're in a rowboat you can pass underneath, which is what I did...twice—the first time going out, the second time coming back in. It was the second time, just as I was emerging from underneath, that I noticed a man on the bridge as I looked up. He was standing in the middle of the bridge with both hands resting on the railing and looking down...at me, I think, but I wasn't sure."

"The prophet?"

"Yes."

"And you didn't see him the first time you passed under the bridge?"

"I don't even know if he was there when I first went through."

"So what happened?"

"I stopped rowing and shouted up at him, 'Is that you?' I just wanted to make sure."

◆◆◆

"Who else could I be but me?" came the response.

"It's definitely you," I said softly.

"And how's your search going, Nouriel?" he asked.

"How does it look like it's going? I'm in a rowboat...on a lake...in Central Park. Not very well."

"But you're in a place of trees."

"Is this the place of our next meeting?"

"I guess it is."

"Then how do we meet?"

"Either you get out of the boat and join me on the bridge, or I get off the bridge and join you in the boat. I'd recommend the latter."

So he came down from the bridge while I navigated the boat to the side to find a place from which he could get in—which he did. It was now me and the prophet...in a rowboat...on a lake...in Central Park. There were several other boats in the water that day, but from the moment he joined me, everything else faded into the background as the focus turned to an ancient mystery and the future of a nation. We could have been anywhere.

◆◆◆

"And you continued rowing as you spoke?"

"Yes...as we spoke...and as I recorded."

––––––◆◆◆––––––

He was quiet for a time. We both were. As the boat neared the middle of the lake, the prophet broke the silence. "So, Nouriel, what have you found so far?"

"The Sixth Harbinger is the sycamore from Isaiah 9:10:

> "But we will rebuild with quarried stone.
> *The sycamores have been cut down.*"

"And why do you think the sycamores would have been cut down?" he asked.

"It had to be the Assyrians in their invasion...part of devastating the land."

"And why would a fallen sycamore be significant?"

"That's as far as I got."

"If the fallen bricks foreshadowed the nation's future collapse, what did the fallen sycamore foreshadow?"

"I don't know."

"It's a sign of uprooting...the uprooting of a kingdom. Do you have the seal, Nouriel?"

I gave it to him. He held it up as he began to reveal its meaning.

"The Sixth Harbinger: The destruction isn't limited to buildings. The enemy's attack causes the sycamore to be cut down. The fallen sycamore is a sign of warning and, in the ignoring of the warning, becomes a prophecy of judgment. The Sixth Harbinger: the sign of uprooting—the Sycamore."

"But what does it have to do with America? The agents of al Qaeda weren't interested in sycamores. And the sycamore of Isaiah 9:10 grows in the Middle East and Africa, not anywhere near the events of 9/11."

"That's true," he said.

"So I don't see how anything could connect. The chances of..."

"The *chances of* don't mean anything."

"What do you mean?"

"In the last moments of the calamity, the North Tower began to collapse. In the midst of that collapse, it sent debris and wreckage through the air toward a plot of land at the border of Ground Zero. It was unlike the other properties surrounding Ground Zero in that it wasn't covered with concrete, steel, or asphalt...but with soil and grass."

I stopped rowing and let the boat glide. He paused for a moment, before continuing.

"The wreckage hurled by the falling tower struck an object."

"An object? What kind of an object?"

"A tree."

"No..."

"After the cloud of dust began to clear, police officers, rescue workers, and onlookers gazed at the little plot of land at the edge of Ground Zero. There in the middle of the ash and debris that covered the ground was a fallen tree. It would soon become a symbol of 9/11 and of Ground Zero. And it *was* a symbol...but one much more ancient than anyone there could have realized, and one carrying a message no one could have fathomed."

"What tree was it?" I asked.

"The tree that was struck down," he answered.

"What kind of tree was it?"

"It was a sycamore tree."

"The tree at Ground Zero that was struck down on September 11..."

"...was a sycamore tree."

"But how?" I asked. "How could it?...They don't grow here."

"When the American leaders declared, '*We will rebuild,*' the same words of Israel's ancient vow, did they proclaim it in ancient Hebrew?"

"No, of course not," I replied.

"And why not?" he asked.

"Because American leaders don't speak ancient Hebrew, and who would have understood it?"

"Exactly. In each case, the ancient and the modern, the leaders speak in the tongue of their people and nation. The Harbinger is translated into the context of the nation in which it appears and to the people to whom it is directed. So too with the sign of the Sycamore. It was a translation."

"A translation...how?"

"The tree matches the nation...the land. The tree of Isaiah 9:10 was endemic to Israel. So the tree of 9/11 was endemic to America."

"But you said it was a sycamore."

"It's classified under the genus *platanus*. But it's known by its common English name...*sycamore*. It *was* a sycamore."

"But..."

"Yes, you were right, Nouriel. The *Middle Eastern* sycamore doesn't naturally grow in the American Northeast. But there exists a version of the sycamore that does—the English sycamore."

"The English sycamore...a translation of the Harbinger."

"And it was the English sycamore that happened to be growing on the little plot of land at the border of Ground Zero."

"And it was named *sycamore* because..."

"Because it was named after the Middle Eastern sycamore."

"So the tree that was struck down on 9/11 was named after the tree of Isaiah 9:10?"

"Yes. The ancient Middle Eastern Harbinger was translated into Western form...into an American tree bearing the same name of the Middle Eastern tree of Israel's judgment."

"And it just happened to be standing there on the corner of Ground Zero on 9/11."

"Just as with everything else," he said, "it just happened to be."

"But the Assyrians intended to cut down the sycamore tree—the terrorists of 9/11 didn't."

"The terrorists had no idea of Isaiah 9:10, no idea of the Harbingers, no idea of the sycamore tree growing at the corner of Ground Zero, and no idea that their attack would cause it to fall or that its fall was connected to an ancient prophecy. They had no idea...but still it happened."

"And what happened after it fell?" I asked.

"It became the focal point of interest and attention. It was transformed into a symbol."

"Just as with the Harbingers before it."

"The Harbingers are, among other things, symbols. So the Sycamore became a symbol of 9/11. It was labeled *the Sycamore of Ground Zero*. Articles were written about it. It was placed on public display. Crowds gathered around to see it. But they had no idea of the message it carried or how far-reaching that message was. Nor did they take note of the small object entwined in its roots."

"Which was..."

"A brick," he replied. "*The bricks have fallen... and the sycamores have been cut down.*"

"The whole thing is... I can't even put it into words... everything replaying itself... everything following the details of an ancient prophecy... now even inanimate objects... the Tower... the Stone... the Tree... and with nobody orchestrating it."

"With nobody orchestrating it because it had to happen. The Harbingers manifested because they *had* to manifest... as signs... as prophetic messages."

"And what message does the sign of the Sycamore hold for America?" I asked.

"It's a sign of a fall... of a cutting down... an uprooting... an end. When it appeared in ancient Israel, it prophesied the nation's downfall and the end of its kingdom."

"And now it reappears for America. So does that mean that there has to be an..."

"It's a warning," said the prophet. "It all depends if the warning is heeded."

"And if it's not heeded...?"

"If a tree falls to the ground and no one hears it... does it make a sound?"

"Does it?" I asked.

"In the case of the Sycamore, it makes two."

"Two?"

"For those who hear it, the sound of warning and the call to redemption."

"And for those who don't?"

"The sound of judgment."

◆◆◆

We were silent for a time. Then he reached into his coat pocket and handed me the next seal. I examined it without saying anything, placed it in my pocket, then resumed rowing to bring the boat back in to the dock. "And what clue do you have for me concerning the Seventh Harbinger?" I asked as we neared the dock.

"It's as clear as the one before it," he replied, "and closely joined."

"Closely joined to the Sycamore."

"Yes."

"It's another image of a tree...but different."

"Correct."

"There are two trees in the prophecy," I said. "So the Seventh Harbinger has to be the second tree."

"You see, Nouriel, it's not so hard. You've already figured out all that and without even spending weeks searching for the answer. And we haven't even reached the dock."

"Then why do we need weeks or months before the next meeting?"

"For you to work on it."

"Why don't we just keep going...here? It's a place of trees. The setting works."

He thought for a moment, then responded. "Why not then?"

"Then we'll do it here?"

"Why not?" he repeated.

I never expected him to agree to the suggestion. It threw me. It threw me enough to question him. "So a prophet can change the plan...the appointed plan?"

"Who said the plan was changed?"

"But I was the one who came up with the idea."

"And how do you know that your coming up with the idea to change the plan wasn't the appointed plan in the first place?"

"If it was a change of plan...then it wasn't appointed."

"And if it was appointed," he replied, "then it wasn't a change of plan."

"So you're saying you planned to continue here all along...before I mentioned it?"

"Whether I planned it or whether it happened because it was planned without my planning it makes no difference."

"I think you're just saying all this."

"And you're free to think that," he replied.

"So I'm *free* to think that. I don't *have* to think that."

"But that doesn't mean it wasn't planned," he added.

"How could it be both?" I asked.

"It takes two oars to make a boat go straight."

"Meaning it's both free will and predestination?"

"Meaning you need to use both oars and focus on keeping the boat straight, so we can make it back to dry land."

Chapter 11

The Seventh Harbinger:
The Erez Tree

א ה

S HE ROSE FROM her chair. "Nouriel, would you excuse me for a moment before we continue?"

"Of course," he answered.

She walked over to her desk. "Is everyone gone?" she asked, speaking into the phone set.

"Yes," replied the voice on the speaker, "Everyone's gone, and I'll be leaving soon."

"You'll make sure everything's turned off?"

"I will."

During the exchange, Nouriel gazed out to the city skyline. It was now early evening. The sun had set. The city was illumined by the deep blues and reds of twilight and the incandescent and fluorescent radiance of its buildings and street lamps.

"So..." she said, as she returned to the round table, "you were in the boat with the prophet..."

"We docked, got out of the boat, and began walking through the park. He led me to the fountain on the terrace, the one with the statue of the angel on top."

◆◆◆

"Do you know what that is, Nouriel?" he asked.

"An angel," I replied.

"This is Bethesda Fountain, and that's called the *Angel of the Waters*. It's from the Gospel of John, the account of a crippled man who waited by the pools of Bethesda in Jerusalem to be healed. And do you know what *Bethesda* means?"

"No," I replied.

"It comes from the Hebrew word *khesed*, which means *mercy* or *loving-kindness. Bethesda* means *the house of mercy* or *the place of loving-kindness. Khesed*…mercy…love. It's God's nature, His essence. Don't forget that, through all this, don't forget that. Judgment is His necessity, but His nature and essence—His heart— is love. He's the one always calling out to the lost to be saved."

We resumed our walk, passing by others in the park also walking or running or playing chess or just sitting on the park benches doing nothing in particular. We followed the walking path through a lush green landscape of trees and grass, rocks and bridges.

"So, Nouriel, if the Sycamore is the Sixth Harbinger, then the Seventh Harbinger…"

"Has to be the cedar. It's what comes next:

> "The sycamores have been cut down,
>   *But we will plant cedars in their place.*"

"Correct."

"So the tree on the seal is a cedar."

"Yes, and what does it mean?"

"I have no idea."

"Their sycamores are fallen. They vow to replace them. But instead of replacing them with other sycamores, they replace them with cedars. Why do you think they would do that?"

"It would have to be for the same reason they didn't replace the fallen bricks with other bricks but with quarried stone. The goal wasn't restoration but defiance. So I'd guess that the cedar was stronger than the sycamore, or as different from the sycamore…"

"…as quarried stones were from clay bricks. You're right. The sycamore was a common tree. It was never seen as something of great value. Its grain was coarse, knotty, spongy, and not particularly strong. And though its wood could be used in construction, it was neither the most ideal nor most durable material to build with."

"So it was kind of the clay brick of trees."

"Exactly. And as the clay bricks were replaced by massive stones, the fallen sycamore would be replaced by the cedar."

"So the cedar was stronger than the sycamore?"

"Much stronger, and much more highly valued. The sycamore grew in the low lands; the cedar grew on mountain heights. The sycamore was common; the cedar was exotic. Unlike the twisting sycamore, the cedar was straight, majestic, and towering. Its wood was smooth, durable, and perfectly suited for construction. The sycamore could reach a height of about fifty feet; but the cedar could grow to well over a hundred. That was the point. They would plant cedars in place of the fallen sycamores. And unlike the sycamore, the cedar would stand strong against any future attack...or so they hoped. One commentary puts it this way:

> "Instead of hearkening, heeding, and repenting, the nation determines to act in a spirit of defiance...*it will exchange its feeble sycamores that are cut down for strong cedars which the wildest gales will spare.*[1]

"The *wildest gales* would be what?" he asked.

"The nation's coming day of judgment," I replied.

"Yes. And on that day nothing would be spared—not the trees, not the stones, not the nation. And the kingdom would fall as quickly and violently as a cedar crashing down to the earth."

"So it's the same thing they did with the quarried stone...the same act in a different form. They laid the quarried stone in the place of fallen bricks. Now they plant the cedar in the place of the sycamore."

"It's the act of *khalaf*," he said.

"*Khalaf*?"

"It's the Hebrew word used in the verse. It means *to exchange, to replace, to plant one thing in the place of another.*"

"And what about the word *cedar*?" I asked. "*Cedar* is English. What's the original word used in the prophecy? What was the tree called in Hebrew?"

"*Erez*. It was called the *erez*. 'The sycamores have fallen, but we will plant *erez trees* in their place.'"

"So *erez* means *cedar*?" I asked.

"Yes and no," he replied. "*Cedar* is the word most often used to translate *erez*, as in the cedars of Lebanon. But *erez* means much more than the English *cedar*. Come." With that, he left the path and led me over to a tree. "How would you describe it, Nouriel?"

"It's an evergreen."

"And what else?"

"It has cones, and its leaves are needlelike."

"It's a coniferous tree, a conifer. The classic botanical work known as *Hierobotanicon* defines the Hebrew *erez* as a conifer or coniferous tree. The word *erez* also appears in several different ancient texts where it refers to an evergreen conifer."

"So an Erez Tree is a coniferous evergreen."

"Yes," he replied, "but not every coniferous evergreen is necessarily an Erez Tree."

"So what exactly is it?" I asked.

"Most specifically it's a *particular kind* of cone-bearing evergreen. One commentator more narrowly pinpoints it:

> "The Hebrew *erez* rendered *cedar* in all English versions, is most likely a generic word for the pine family."[2]

"And that means what...exactly?"

"The Erez Tree would fall under the botanical classification of *pinacea*."

"*Pinacea*. And what," I asked, "does *pinacea* refer to specifically?"

"The cedar, the spruce, the pine, and the fir."

"So the most accurate identification of the Hebrew word *erez* would be *pinacea tree*."

"Yes. The most botanically precise translation of the vow would be, 'But we will plant *pinacea trees* in their place.'"

"And the pinacea includes the cedar, but more than the cedar."

"Correct. So they plant the stronger tree in place of the weaker, as they vow a stronger nation to replace a weaker one. The Erez Tree becomes another symbol of the nation and its defiance—a living symbol of their confidence in their national resurgence, their tree of hope."

"A tree of hope, but not a good hope."

"No," he replied, "a prideful, self-centered, and godless hope. What they saw as a tree of hope was, in reality, a harbinger of judgment."

He asked me for the seal. So, of course, I gave it to him, and, lifting it up in his right hand, as he had done with the others, he began to reveal its mystery.

"The Seventh Harbinger: The warning of the fallen sycamore goes unheeded. Its uprooted remains are removed. Another tree is brought to the place of its fall, a Hebrew erez, a conifer, an evergreen, the biblical cedar—the pinacea tree. The Erez Tree is planted in the same spot where the fallen Sycamore had once stood. The planting is vested with symbolic meaning. The second tree becomes a symbol of national resurgence, confidence, and hope. But like the quarried stone, in reality, it embodies the nation's defiance. It will stand as a witness of a nation's false hope and a living omen of its rejection of the warning given…the Seventh Harbinger—the Erez Tree."

"So the sign is the appearance of the Erez Tree."

"Yes."

"Its planting."

"Yes, its planting, and in the place of the fallen Sycamore."

"If that happens, the Seventh Harbinger is manifested."

"Yes."

At that point, we resumed our walking.

"And has the Seventh Harbinger manifested?" I asked.

"It has."

"How?"

"It began with the removing of the Sycamore."

"The Sycamore of Ground Zero."

"Yes. It was taken from the place of its fall and put on public display as a symbol of the calamity. Even its root system would be carefully removed and transferred to another site."

"But for the ancient mystery to play out," I said, "another tree would have to be brought to the same plot of land and planted in the same place where the Sycamore had stood."

"In late November of 2003, two years after the fall of the Sycamore, a strange sight appeared at the corner of Ground Zero—in the sky…a tree. It was being transported by crane over a courtyard of soil and grass. Those in charge of the operation carefully guided it down to the appointed spot. The new tree was set into position to stand on the same spot where once had stood the Sycamore of Ground Zero."

"What was it? What kind of tree?"

"The most natural thing to have done would have been to replace the one Sycamore with another. But the prophecy required that the fallen Sycamore be replaced with a tree of an entirely different nature. So the tree that replaced the Sycamore of Ground Zero was likewise *not* a sycamore. According to the prophecy, the Sycamore must be replaced by the biblical *erez*. So it must be replaced by a conifer tree."

"And the tree that replaced the Sycamore of Ground Zero…?"

"The tree that replaced the Sycamore was a conifer tree."

"An evergreen?"

"Yes…with needlelike leaves and cones.

"They replaced the fallen Sycamore with the Erez Tree!"

"The sign of a nation's false hope and defiance before God."

"It's like something out of a movie…it's surreal!"

"Except that it's real."

"Who was behind the decision to do that?" I asked.

"No one," he answered. "No one in the sense of any one person making it all happen or trying to fulfill the prophecy."

"No one had any idea what they were doing?"

"No one."

"Then where did it come from?"

"The tree was a gift donated from an outside party, just as was the Gazit Stone that replaced the fallen bricks."

"But you narrowed the word *erez* down more specifically to one particular kind of conifer."

"The pinacea tree."

"And the tree that was lowered into the ground...?"

"Its Latin name was *picea albies*."

"And..."

"The tree that replaced the Sycamore was a pinacea tree."

"A pinacea tree! The same tree of the ancient prophecy...the same tree that *had* to replace the fallen sycamore...Unbelievable!"

"And the sister tree to the Cedar of Lebanon."

"And it all took place at the corner of Ground Zero?"

"Yes."

"And the replacing of the bricks with the Gazit Stone happened at Ground Zero."

"Yes."

"So both parts of the ancient prophecy were fulfilled in the same place...at Ground Zero."

"And not only in the same place," he said, "but in the same way."

"What do you mean?"

"They didn't just place a Gazit Stone on Ground Zero. They made it into a public event, a public gathering completely centered around the Harbinger. So it was with the replacing of the Sycamore by the Erez Tree. The act became a public event, a gathering completely centered on the Harbinger."

"And who led the event?"

"A local spiritual leader."

"So the planting of the Erez Tree was made into a ceremony?"

"A ceremony centered on the act of replacement, as the laying down of the Gazit Stone was an act of replacement. Each event centered on one of the Harbingers. Neither had anything to do with repentance; instead, each exalted the human spirit and its defiance of calamity. It was another echo of the ancient vow. Two and half thousand years earlier, the people of Israel responded to their calamity by planting the Erez Tree as a sign of their defiant, self-confident hope. Now, in the aftermath of 9/11 and against the backdrop of Ground Zero, the assembled New Yorkers repeated the ancient act with their new Erez Tree. They too transformed it into a sign. During that ceremony, the officiant bestowed on the tree a name. He proclaimed:

"This *Ground Zero Tree of Hope* will be a sign of the indomitable nature of human hope...[3]

"A tree of hope," said the prophet.

"And *a sign*."

"Yes, of the indomitable nature. *Indomitable*...meaning *unconquerable*."

"The spirit of the vow."

"And in the vow, what word was used for this act?"

"You just told me...*khalaf*."

"Which means?"

"To exchange, to replace, to plant something in the place of another."

"So that's exactly what has to be fulfilled. It's not just that one tree is fallen and a new one planted—but the new tree has to be planted in the *same place*. The Erez Tree must be planted in the *same place* where the fallen Sycamore had once stood. Now listen to the words they proclaimed that day as they gathered around the Erez Tree:

"The Tree of Hope is planted *in the very spot where* a sixty-year-old *sycamore stood* the morning of September 11, 2001."[4]

"And nobody realized that what they were doing was matching up with the prophecy?" I asked. "There was no one putting it all together?"

"No one," he answered.

"It's an exact, precise fulfillment of the ancient vow. It's exact, and as if they're highlighting it so you can't miss it."

"That's the nature of the Harbingers, Nouriel. They have to be made manifest."

"They couldn't have matched it any more precisely than if they had recited Isaiah 9:10 word for word. And nobody was trying to make it happen. They all just happened to do it?"

"Think about it, Nouriel. Who could have put it all together? The tower fell because of the terrorists. It happened to fall exactly as it did in order to strike down that one particular tree. The tree just happened to be a sycamore, which just happened to be growing at the corner of Ground Zero. The tree that would replace it just happened to be given as a gift from outsiders who had nothing to do with anything else, but who just happened to feel led to give it. Their gift just happened to be the fulfillment of the biblical Erez Tree, which just happened to be the same tree spoken of in the ancient vow—the tree that must replace the Sycamore. They just happened to lower it into the same soil in that the fallen Sycamore had once stood—exactly as in the Hebrew of the ancient vow. And the man who led the ceremony around the tree just happened to bring it all together without knowing that he was bringing anything together. No one knew what they were doing. It wasn't a matter of intent. It was the manifestation of the Harbingers."

"It's mind-boggling," I said, "and another replaying of the mystery. They were all stepping into the ancient footsteps—and they thought it was their own."

"It *was* their own," he said, "but in the ancient footsteps."

"Another piece of an ancient puzzle falling into place, another reenactment of an ancient drama…of judgment. It still seems like a movie. It's still hard to believe that it's all real, that it actually happened."

"It all happened…and is happening."

"And what's the message of the Erez Tree?"

"The same message it carried to ancient Israel. The Ground Zero Tree of Hope was a sign, as it was proclaimed to be, but not of the hope they proclaimed. Instead, it was the sign of a nation's defiant rejection of God's call to return."

"And concerning the future…what does it mean?"

"When you see the Erez Tree planted in the place of the fallen Sycamore, it's an omen, a warning. What does it mean for the future? One commentary on Isaiah 9:10 puts it this way:

> "'If the enemy cut down the sycamores, we will *plant cedars in the room of them*. We will make a hand of God's judgments, gain by them, and so outbrave them.' Note, those are ripening

apace for ruin whose hearts are unhumbled under humbling providences."[5]

"*Ripening apace for ruin.* Then there's no hope?" I asked.

"There *is* hope," said the prophet, "but when a nation such as this places its hope in its own powers to save itself, then its hope is false. Its true hope is found only in returning to God. Without that, its Tree of Hope is a harbinger of the day when its strong cedars come crashing down to the earth."

◆◆◆

He stopped walking. "And now, Nouriel, we approach the last Harbingers...the last two...each as closely joined to the other as the Erez Tree is to the Sycamore."

He handed me the next seal, the seal of the Eighth Harbinger, which I promptly examined. It's image was of some kind of platform...some kind of wide, low platform. I couldn't make anything of it beyond that.

"You're puzzled," he said as he saw my reaction.

"Yes," I replied. "This one doesn't look too promising."

"What else do you have to go on?"

"The words of the vow. But the vow *ends* with the planting of the Erez Tree, the cedar. There's nothing more."

"And what other clues do you have?"

"I don't know."

"You forgot the other clues? There are only two left. It's a simple process of deduction. One is of stone..."

"The Gazit Stone," I replied."

"The other is fallen..."

"The bricks...The bricks are fallen."

"One ascends..."

"It has to be the Tower."

"One is alive..."

"The Erez Tree."

"And the other one was..."

"The Sycamore."

"There are only two left," he said.

"Tell me again," I replied.

"One speaks of what is, and the other of what would be."

"One speaks of what is, and the other of what would be. Very mystical…and vague."

"The last two Harbingers are not like the others," he said, "and yet like all of them."

"Not like the others and yet like all of them. I have to suppose you believe you're helping me."

"I am," he replied.

"I need something more."

"You're right. The last two are harder than the rest."

"That's the clue?" I asked.

"And not here, but far away."

"Far away…Far away like the mountain?"

"Yes."

"As far?" I asked.

"About as far," he replied.

"That doesn't narrow it down much."

"The prophecy will reveal it."

"Where it is?"

"Yes."

"I don't see how."

"Until then," he said, and then left me there at the edge of the park.

I shouted after him, "You could at least say, 'Good luck, you'll be needing it.'"

"But I don't believe in luck, Nouriel," he replied without turning back. He began crossing the street in a crowd of other pedestrians. I made my way to the start of the crossing but went no farther.

"But if I don't know what I'm looking for," I shouted, "how will I know it when I see it?"

"You won't," he answered.

"I won't know it?"

"No, you won't see it."

"And why not?"

He reached the other side of the street, stopped, and turned around to face me.

"Why won't you see it?" he shouted across the street.

"Yes," I shouted.

"Because you can't see it...It's invisible, of course."

He then turned around, resumed his walking, and disappeared into the crowd.

Chapter 12

The Eighth Harbinger: The Utterance

א ה

S o," SHE SAID with a slight smile of amusement, "you were now on a journey to find an invisible harbinger."

"Exactly," he answered, "an invisible harbinger based on an unidentifiable image."

"An unidentifiable image on the seal…"

"Yes."

"What about the other clues?"

"Like *one speaks of what is… and the other of what would be*?"

"Yes."

"What could I do with that? What was it revealing?"

"He gave you other clues though."

"He told me that the last two Harbingers were *unlike the others… and yet like all of them*."

"And was that a help?"

"Does it sound like a help?"

"Not a lot of help… no."

"The most I could get out of it was that each of the Harbingers had to do with one piece of the mystery, but the last two wouldn't be about one piece but about the mystery as a whole—not like *any* of the others and yet like *all* of them."

"Sounds plausible enough."

"Yes, but still leading me nowhere."

"What about the vow? Up to that point, everything was following the vow. Everything was taking place in order."

"There was nothing left. You had the Bricks, the Tower, the Gazit Stone, the Sycamore, and the Erez Tree. It ended with, *But we will plant cedars in their place.* There was nothing else in the verse to give any clues."

"What about it being far away?"

"That was the one clue that actually gave me something to go on."

"How?"

"I asked him if it was as far away as the mountain. He answered that it was just about as far."

"Pretty general."

"Still, it was something to go on. The mountain was about four hours away from the city. So the same distance would be..."

"But *about as far,*" she said, "isn't equivalent to saying it's the same distance."

"Still," he replied, "it *could* be the same distance. In any case, to be safe, I allowed a distance of three to five hours from the city. That's a few hundred miles. Then I drew a circle around it."

"With New York City in the center?"

"Yes, to a radius of a few hundred miles, to see what it would include."

"There had to have been a lot of places."

"There were—New York State, New Jersey, Connecticut, Pennsylvania, Massachusetts, Maryland, Delaware..."

"But how could that possibly lead you to find the Eighth Harbinger? It would be a needle in a haystack."

"It couldn't lead me...not without something else. But the prophet gave me one more clue. He said, '*The prophecy will reveal it.*' So I looked again at the prophecy for something that could give me a clue to the place."

"And...?"

"The only thing that I hadn't considered was the introduction:

"The LORD sent a word against Jacob,
And it has fallen on Israel.
All the people will know—
Ephraim and the inhabitants of Samaria—
Who say in pride and arrogance of heart:
'The bricks have fallen down...'"[1]

"How could you find a clue in that?" she asked.

The names," he replied. "Ephraim, Jacob, Samaria—they were all linked to Israel."

"So the Eighth Harbinger was in Israel?"

"No. Israel isn't exactly four hours away. I searched the commentaries to see what they had to say...if they could lead me to the missing key."

"And did they?"

"Yes."

"So what was it?"

"It was Samaria."

"Samaria? Isn't that almost the same as saying *Israel*?"

"It depends. *Samaria* wasn't just another name for the kingdom of Israel. It was also the name of a city. The prophecy is directed at those who dwell in Samaria. Was it Samaria the kingdom or Samaria the city...or both?"

"I have no idea," she replied. "But why would that be important?"

"The vow could've been spoken anywhere in the land and by anyone. It could have become a rallying cry or an anthem among the people. But it would only be significant if it represented the response of the entire nation. And who can speak for an entire nation?"

"The leaders?"

"Exactly. So Samaria was the nation's capital city, the seat of its government, the city of its kings and officials. For the vow to matter, it had to be spoken by the leaders; it had to be the nation's official response. So it had to be proclaimed in the capital city. And then I discovered a clue in one of the commentaries on Isaiah 9:10 that linked the vow to the nation's capital:

"National pride is usually most arrogant in a capital city.[2]

"It's the key. The vow has to be proclaimed in the capital city. That's what I was looking for—the capital city." He paused, waiting for her to get it.

"Washington DC?" she said.

"What were the two targets of 9/11?" he asked.

"New York City and Washington."

"It was already connected."

"What about the distance?" she asked. "Did it fall inside the radius?"

"Washington is just a little over four hours from New York City—the same distance as to the mountain. So if I was right, there would be some connection between Washington DC and the words of the vow. If I was right, then somewhere in the capital city was the Eighth Harbinger. So that's where I had to go."

"But how would you know where to go once you got there?" she asked.

"I wouldn't...anymore than I knew where to go the other times. I just went on what I knew...or what I thought I knew."

"So where did you go?"

"First to the Pentagon, the place with the most direct connection to 9/11. But my access was limited, of course, and nothing seemed to connect. The following day I went to the White House. But again, no connection. After that I went to the Lincoln Memorial."

"What was it about the Lincoln Memorial that you thought would connect?"

"Nothing," he replied. "But I always wanted to see it. And since I was in the neighborhood, I figured if I kept searching, I would end up in the place I was supposed to end up in, one way or another. So it was as good a place as any."

"And...?"

I'd never been there before. It was impressive up close—massive marble columns like some Greek temple and, of course, the statue, larger than life...noble...powerful. I was staring at his face when I heard it...from behind."

◆◆◆

"Considered the greatest of American presidents," said the voice.

I turned around. It was the prophet. Before I could acknowledge his presence, he spoke again.

"And perhaps the most sorrowful," he said. "Even in stone, it comes through."

"So I'm here," I said. "I made it."

"You did, Nouriel. I'm impressed. But I knew you would." He led me over the side to look at the words engraved on the wall. "Lincoln's Second Inaugural Address," he said, and then began to read the words out loud:

> "The Almighty has His own purposes....Fondly do we hope, fervently do we pray, that this mighty scourge of war may speedily pass away. Yet, if God wills that it continue until all the wealth piled by the bondsman's two hundred and fifty years of unrequited toil shall be sunk, and until every drop of blood drawn with the lash shall be paid by another drawn with the sword, as was said three thousand years ago, so still it must be said, that the judgments of the Lord are true and righteous altogether."[3]

He paused and turned to see my reaction. "Do you understand what it's saying, Nouriel?"

"That behind the war that was devastating the nation..."

"Was judgment...a national judgment for the sin of slavery: *'Until every drop of blood drawn with the lash shall be paid by another drawn with the sword.'*"

"And so his sadness," I said quietly.

"But lying behind the judgment were the purposes of redemption, that slavery would be removed from the land."

"The Almighty has His own purposes."

"Yes, *the Almighty has His own purposes.*" He began walking toward the entrance but stopped just short of the steps where he stood silhouetted against the sunlight outside the memorial, framed between two colossal marble columns. He was waiting for me to join him. And I did. So we both stood there between the columns, looking out toward the reflecting pool, the mall, and the obelisk of the Washington Monument in the distance.

"So, tell me, Nouriel, how did you know? How did you know it was Washington?"

"It was Samaria," I said, "the capital city. The vow had to be spoken in the capital city."

"And why would that be?"

"Because the capital city is the seat of the government, the place from which the nation is led. The vow only matters if it represents the will or voice of the nation, if it's the nation's response to God. And only the leaders can speak for the nation as a whole."

"Well done, Nouriel. So what would we expect to find in Washington DC?"

"Some link between this city and the ancient vow," I said. "Somehow Isaiah 9:10 has to be connected to Washington DC."

"Correct. In the days of Isaiah the vow would undoubtedly have been spoken or repeated throughout the land. But the vow is proclaimed with authority and on behalf of the entire nation. It sums up the nation's response and sets forth its future course. Whatever else it may have been, the vow had to have been a public declaration of the nation's leaders. It had to be proclaimed somehow in the capital city."

"And so the Eighth Harbinger is what exactly?" I asked.

"What's left in Isaiah 9:10 that hasn't yet been revealed as one of the Nine Harbingers?"

"Nothing. It ends with the planting of the Erez Tree."

"Nothing?" he said. "Then everything."

"What do you mean?" I asked.

"I told you that the last Harbingers are unlike the others and yet like all of them. What did you make of that?"

"That they wouldn't be so much about the individual pieces of the puzzle but about the whole."

"Correct again. And what else did I tell you?"

"That I wouldn't see them... that they were invisible."

"So put the clues together."

"It's about the whole."

"The whole of what?" he asked.

"The whole of the mystery."

"And more specifically...?"

"The whole of Isaiah 9:10...the whole of the vow."

"So what then is the Eighth Harbinger?"

"Isaiah 9:10?"

"And when is Isaiah 9:10 invisible?"

"When it's spoken?"

"Correct."

"So the Eighth Harbinger is Isaiah 9:10 in spoken form?"

"The Eighth Harbinger is the vow itself proclaimed by the nation's leaders in the capital city—the spirit of defiance given voice, the pronouncement of judgment."

"The nation's leaders pronouncing judgment on their nation?"

"Unwittingly...by publicly proclaiming the vow, they seal the nation's course, and by so doing pronounce judgment on the land. I assume you brought the seal with you?"

I took it out of my pocket and handed it to him.

"Were you able to figure out the image?" he asked.

"No."

"It's a platform," he said, "a speaker's platform...from which, in ancient times, leaders and orators would address their audiences."

Then he lifted the seal in his right hand and began revealing its meaning. "The Eighth Harbinger: In the aftermath of the calamity, the nation's leaders respond with public proclamations of defiance. They boast of the nation's resolve and power. They speak of its fallen bricks and quarried stones, its uprooted trees and their replanting. They speak of a nation defiant and resolved to emerge stronger than before. The words take the form of a vow. The vow gives voice to a national spirit and seals the nation's course. It all takes place in the capital city. The Eighth Harbinger: the Utterance."

The prophet stepped out from between the columns and descended a few of the marble stairs...then sat down. I followed and sat down beside him.

"It was the third year after the calamity," he said.

"Israel's calamity," I asked, "or America's?"

"It was the third year after 9/11. The pieces of the ancient puzzle were falling into place. In late November of 2003, the Erez Tree was lowered into the earth to replace the fallen Sycamore. On the following Fourth of July, 2004, the Gazit Stone was, in turn, lowered to the floor of Ground Zero to replace the fallen Bricks. So by the summer of 2004, every object mentioned in the ancient prophecy had manifested, and each at Ground Zero. Less than three months later would come the manifestation of the Eighth Harbinger."

"But not at Ground Zero."

"No, in the nation's capital where the nation's leaders reside. According to the mystery, it would have to involve at least one leader, one who could speak on behalf of the nation…a figure of national prominence. He would have to utter words paralleling the ancient vow."

"And all this would have to take place publicly."

"Yes. In the autumn of 2004, the nation was in the final stage of a presidential election. The candidate campaigning on the Democratic ticket for the office of vice presidency, a member of the Senate, was, at that time, among the most prominent of the nation's leaders. It was September 11, 2004. The vice presidential candidate had been invited to speak at a gathering of a congressional caucus in the nation's capital on the anniversary of the calamity. It would be an eloquent address, designed to inspire its hearers. *It would also be a sign.* What would proceed out of his mouth would be even more precise and more eerie than that which had been spoken over the stone at Ground Zero. September 11, 2004, the third anniversary of the calamity, these are the exact words spoken that day in Washington DC, the nation's capital city:

> "Good morning. Today, on this day of remembrance and mourning, we have the Lord's word to get us through:
>
> *The bricks have fallen*
> *But we will build with dressed stones*
> *The sycamores have been cut down*
> *But we will put cedars in their place.*"[4]

"My God!" I said. "That's too…"

"It is," said the prophet. "Nevertheless, it happened."

"I can't believe…"

"But it happened."

"He said those exact words?"

"Those…exact…words."

"But it's a prophecy of judgment! What was he doing proclaiming…"

"That's the point."

"He proclaimed Isaiah 9:10…"

"The code to the Harbingers."

"It's too much…"

"But it's real."

◆◆◆

Ana had been silent up to this point, just trying to take it all in. But she could no longer contain her reaction. "It's totally unbelievable…" she said. "It's like something out of a…"

"I know," he replied, "but it's all real."

"When the prophet told you all these things, did you check them out to verify them, to make sure they actually happened?" she asked.

"Yes," he replied.

"And they all checked out?"

"Yes, they all checked out."

"It's so hard to believe it. Now it's the vice presidential candidate saying it outright…this ancient mystery. It's beyond real."

"I know. I told him that. But it's all true."

"But why would anyone proclaim that vow?" she asked.

"I asked the same thing of the prophet."

"And what was his answer?"

"His answer was that it happened for the same reason everything else happened. It wasn't about the motive or the intention of the one doing it, but the fact that it was done…that it happened. It happened because it *had* to happen. It was another replaying of the ancient mystery. What the speaker intended to say was irrelevant.

The words came out because those were the words that had to be spoken. The vow *had* to be proclaimed, the words of the ancient leaders over the ancient calamity *had* to be proclaimed by an American leader over 9/11. And by doing so, the two nations, the ancient and the modern, were bound together. The utterance would join the Assyrian invasion to 9/11 and America's post-9/11 defiance to Israel's defiance in the face of God's judgment."

"But how," she asked, "did it happen that the vice presidential candidate could end up saying those words?"

"That's the same thing I wanted to know. I asked the prophet how many verses there were in the Bible."

◆◆◆

"Over thirty thousand," he told me.

"So," I replied, "out of over thirty thousand verses...that's the one he chose? And you said it was obscure...that even people who read the Bible every day would probably have no idea it existed."

"That is correct," he replied.

"So how on earth did he end up choosing that particular verse?"

"How was the Sycamore cut down?" he asked. "Through a series of twists and quirks. But now the twists and quirks take place in the realm of speech writing, in the searching through quotations deemed most appropriate for such occasions, in the borrowing of passages and quotes from other proclamations and speeches. It doesn't matter how it happened; the point is *it happened*. One of the most prominent of American leaders had now proclaimed the ancient vow—one of the most obscure verses in the Bible and one of the most ominous."

"And he too had no idea what he was doing...or saying?" I asked.

"If he had, he never would have done it."

"It's *stunning*..."

"Yes," he said. "It's stunning enough for Isaiah 9:10 to appear in a speech centered on 9/11. But that wasn't the end of it. It wasn't only that the ancient prophecy *appeared* in the speech..."

"What else was it?"

"It was that *the entire speech* actually emanated out of the ancient prophecy and revolved around it."

"The whole speech revolved around Isaiah 9:10?" I asked.

"It was the cornerstone on which the speech was built."

"So an American leader built an entire speech on an ancient vow spoken in defiance of God by the rebellious leaders of a doomed nation?"

"And lest the connection be missed, he proceeded to join the ancient words of judgment to America."

"How?"

"He said this:

> "Let me show you how *we are building and putting cedars* in those three hallowed places.[5]

"And again:

> "And in a place where smoke once rose, you and I, *we will see that cedar rising.*[6]

"And yet again:

> "You will see that while *those bricks fell and the sycamores cut down, our people are making those cedars rise.*"[7]

"He's actually linking the fallen bricks of Ground Zero to the fallen bricks of Israel's judgment!"

"Yes, Nouriel. That's exactly what he's doing. But he doesn't stop there. He speaks as well of fallen sycamores and rising stones..."

"The Gazit Stone."

"Yes, and rising cedars."

"The Erez Tree."

"And all referring to America's campaign to defy the calamity of 9/11, as he links it all to the judgment of ancient Israel. And then he crowns the address with a dramatic conclusion in the form of a final vow:

"The cedars will rise, the stones will go up, and this season of hope will endure."[8]

"And he never realized it?" I asked. "He had absolutely no idea what he was doing?"

"His only intention was to deliver an inspiring speech, a word to encourage a nation. But instead..."

"But instead, he was pronouncing judgment on a nation."

"Yes," said the prophet. "Without realizing the ramifications of his words, he was pronouncing judgment on America."

"Amazing!"

"But so it was in the ancient case as well. Without realizing what they were doing, the leaders of ancient Israel were pronouncing judgment on *their* nation."

"But now it's two and half thousand years later," I said. "Now there's a context—the Book of Isaiah. It's clearly not a word of encouragement. So it means nobody took the time to look even two verses back or ahead to see that it was actually a proclamation of judgment?"

"No, because it *had* to be proclaimed. And yet notice, Nouriel, the senator made a subtle change. The original vow speaks in the future tense—'We *will* rebuild.' 'We *will* plant cedars.' But in the speech, it becomes, 'We *are* building.' 'We *are* making those cedars rise.' Only at the end does it go back to the future tense, 'The cedars *will* rise.' 'The stones *will* go up.' Why do you think that is?"

"When he speaks in the future tense, he's vowing...it's the vow. But when he speaks in the present tense, he's bearing witness to the fact that the vow is being carried out."

"Exactly. He's bearing witness that the vow is being carried out. And to do that, he takes hewn stones and cedars, the symbols of Israel's defiance in Isaiah 9:10, and transforms them into the symbols of America's campaign to rebuild itself after 9/11."

"Just as the actual physical harbingers were literally transformed into the symbols of American resurgence."

"Correct."

"Did he know it was happening?"

"Did he know *what* was happening?"

"Did he know that what he was declaring, figuratively and symbolically, was actually taking place *in reality*? He spoke of the falling of the sycamore as a symbol of 9/11. Did he know that it had actually happened, that a sycamore had actually been struck down on 9/11? And when he spoke of Americans putting up stones and cedars, did he realize that too had actually taken place? Did he know about the Gazit Stone or the Erez Tree?"

"He was only speaking poetically. He had no idea. And even if someone was to report it to him, he still would have had no idea what it all meant, no more idea of what he was doing than those who actually replaced the fallen Sycamore with the Erez Tree, and bricks with stone. Everyone was unknowingly performing their part of the mystery. And his part was to take the ancient vow and transform it. In his address, it ceased to be a quote. It was no longer Israel boasting in its cedars. It was now America. It was thus now America's vow. Everything was being transposed—the Bricks, the Quarried Stone, the Sycamore, the Cedar, and now an American leader was publicly proclaiming the exact words of the vow and bearing witness of its fulfillment, a Harbinger to seal the other Harbingers, and to reveal America as a nation under the shadow of judgment."

"An American leader pronouncing judgment on America!"

"Without realizing it…yes…as the manifestation of the Harbinger."

"So on the anniversary of 9/11, an American leader proclaims the ancient vow…pronounces judgment on his own nation, and he has no idea what he's doing or saying. As with all the other Harbingers, he doesn't intend it or realize what he's doing. Nobody does. And yet it still all happens according to the ancient prophecy….Every piece of the puzzle falls into its exact place, but no one intends it to happen. No human hand directs it. It just happens. I still can't fathom it."

The prophet paused before responding, then spoke, almost in a whisper. "The Almighty," said the prophet, "has His own purposes."

◆◆◆

He reached into his coat pocket and handed me the next seal. "This is the last one," he said, "the seal of the Ninth Harbinger and the last of the Harbingers."

"Do I get a clue?" I asked.

"You already have a clue."

"*Not like the other Harbingers... and yet like all of them?*"

"Yes."

"So then the Ninth Harbinger is like the Eighth Harbinger?" I asked.

"Like and unlike it."

"Is there a law," I asked, "that if something isn't confusing enough as it is, you're required to make it more confusing?"

He didn't answer that.

"So the Ninth Harbinger is like the Eighth Harbinger in that it's a summation of all the Harbingers that went before it?" I asked.

"Yes and no," he answered.

"Do you see what I mean?" I said, as if expecting him to commiserate with my plight.

"Yes," he answered, "it is a summation. But no, not primarily of that which went *before* it."

"Then of what?" I asked.

"Of that which came *after* it."

"How could it be a summation of what came after it?"

"The clue you were given—*One speaks of what is... and the other...*"

"The other," I said, "*the other of what would be.*"

"What is it that you see on the seal?" he asked.

"It looks like... it could be some sort... some sort of document."

"It *is* a document. It's a parchment, the kind on which the Scriptures were written, the kind on which the prophecies of Isaiah were recorded."

"So the Ninth Harbinger is a document?"

"It is," he said, "but not primarily."

"Then what primarily?"

"What is it that speaks of *what would be*, Nouriel?"

"A prophecy," I answered."

"The Ninth Harbinger."

"Is a prophecy?"

"Correct."

"Then we have to look for a prophet?"

"No."

"Then for what?"

He rose to his feet and began walking down the steps. "Come, Nouriel, and I'll show you."

"Show me...?"

"The place where it all happened."

Chapter 13

The Ninth Harbinger: The Prophecy

א ה

WE WALKED DOWN the marble steps and then along the Reflecting Pool.

"A question," I said, breaking the silence.

"Ask," he replied.

"The Ninth Harbinger is *like* the eighth in that it doesn't so much concern a piece of the mystery...of Isaiah 9:10...but the whole...the whole prophecy."

"Yes."

"But it's *different* from the eighth in that the eighth speaks primarily of *what is,* in the present tense, and the ninth speaks about *what would be,* in the future tense. Is that right?"

"Correct."

"Why is that important...the distinction?"

"Because Isaiah 9:10 exists in two realms. In one realm, it's the voice of a nation proclaiming *a vow* in defiance of God. But in the other realm, it's the voice of a prophet, the voice of Isaiah, and of God speaking through him. It's *a prophecy.* And as a prophecy it's a judgment on the nation's defiance and arrogance, and a warning, a sign foretelling its future. It's a message sent from God and in such a way as to fall on the entire nation, so that *all the people will know it.*"

"So the Ninth Harbinger is a manifestation of Isaiah 9:10 in the form of a prophecy."

"As both a vow *and* a prophecy," he said, "and given in such a way as to fall on the nation."

"So then to fall on America."

"Yes."

We walked on for a time in silence as I pondered his words. Then he came to a stop and asked me for the seal he had just given me. Upon receiving it, he began to reveal its mystery.

"The Ninth Harbinger," he said. "In the wake of the calamity, the nation issues its response in the form of a vow. The vow sets the nation on a course of defiance, a course that ends in judgment. The words of the vow become part of a prophetic revelation given to the nation as a whole, an indictment of its rebellion, a foretelling of its future, a warning of its judgment. The Ninth Harbinger: the Prophecy."

"Then according to the mystery there would have to have been a prophetic word given in the wake of 9/11... to fall on the nation."

He didn't answer, but just kept walking.

"A prophecy given, but not by a prophet?"

Still he was silent.

"And the words of the prophecy came true?"

He stopped. "Look at that," he said, pointing forward.

In the distance ahead of us was the massive dome of the Capitol Building.

"The center of the American government," he said.

"Is that the place?" I asked.

He didn't answer but resumed walking. We continued until we reached the foot of the Capitol steps, where we came to a stop.

"Nouriel, when do you think the leaders of ancient Israel first uttered their vow of defiance?"

"Probably right after the calamity."

"And what would *right after the calamity* be with regard to America?"

"The time right after 9/11."

"Like September 12?"

"That *would* be right after. Why?"

"On September 12, 2001," he said, "the morning after the attack, the United States Senate and House of Representatives convened to issue a joint resolution responding to 9/11. It was to be the nation's first official response to the calamity."

"So it was *here*," I said.

"The vow must be spoken on behalf of the entire nation. Here where the nation's representatives gather, the two representative bodies of the American Congress, here would be the most perfect place for it to happen."

"The House of Representatives and the Senate."

"And of the two, the Senate is the upper or highest of representative bodies. And the highest representative of the highest body is the Senate majority leader, the highest representative of the nation's highest representative body, in position to deliver the nation's response to the calamity."

We began ascending the marble steps.

"On the morning after September 11," he said, "America would issue its response to the calamity in the form of a joint resolution of Congress. The one appointed to present the nation's response was the Senate majority leader. The act would be critical. For as a nation responds to a divine warning, its future is determined."

Finally we reached the top of the stairs where the prophet continued his account.

"The smoke still hovered over Ground Zero as the American government prepared to deliver its response to 9/11 before a nation and a world waiting to see what that response would be. The Senate majority leader made his way to the podium on the Senate floor to present it. 'Mr. President,' he said, 'I sent a resolution to the desk.' The assistant legislative clerk then read the document:

> "A joint resolution expressing the sense of the Senate and
> the House of Representatives regarding the terrorist attacks
> launched against the United States on September 11, 2001.[1]

"The clerk continued the reading of the resolution, a condemnation of the attacks, an expression of condolences, and then a call for unity, a war against terrorism, and the punishment of those responsible for the attack and all who assisted them."

"That would all be expected," I said.

"It *would* be," said the prophet. "But then the Senate majority leader began his address. At the end of the speech would come the climax. These are the words proclaimed by the Senate majority leader on Capitol Hill, the morning after 9/11, to present and sum up the nation's response to the calamity. Listen...

> "I know that there is only the smallest measure of inspiration that can be taken from this devastation, but there is a passage in the Bible from Isaiah that I think speaks to all of us at times like this...

> *The bricks have fallen down,*
> *But we will rebuild with dressed stone;*
> *The fig trees have been felled,*
> *But we will replace them with cedars.*[2]

"I was speechless for several moments. I don't know what I expected to hear, but what I heard left me without words and with my heart racing. I was completely stunned. The ancient vow had actually been proclaimed to the nation from Capitol Hill—the vow of fallen bricks and sycamores had echoed through the halls of the United States Congress, and all on the morning after 9/11."

"How?" I asked. "How could that have happened?"

"How could it have happened with the vice presidential candidate, or with the stone or the tree? How could any of it have happened? It had to happen, and so it did."

"But he was identifying America as a nation under judgment."

"Yes, unwittingly."

"The majority leader of the United States Senate was publicly pronouncing judgment on America."

"Blindly," he replied, "having no idea what he was pronouncing. As far as he knew, he was only delivering an inspiring speech."

"But unknowingly playing his part in a prophetic mystery."

"Yes...and so the words of the ancient vow were now officially joined to America and 9/11. And just as Isaiah's recording of the vow transformed it into a matter of national record and a prophetic word for *all the people*, so now the same words were now officially recorded in the Annals of Congress as a matter of national record."

"But the Senate majority leader wasn't a prophet."

"No."

"But you said it's a prophecy. How can someone who isn't a prophet bring forth a prophetic word?"

"In the Gospel of John," he replied, "the eleventh chapter, the high priest Caiaphas is recorded as saying, 'It is necessary that one man should die for the people.' It was the beginning of the plot that would end with the crucifixion of the Messiah. But it was something else as well. It was also a prophecy, namely, that one man, Jesus, would die for the people, to save them. Caiaphas wasn't a prophet. He was an ungodly man, and yet he prophesied. It wasn't the man— it was the office he held. He was speaking, as the Gospel puts it, 'not of his own initiative,' but prophesying by virtue of his office, as the chief representative of the nation."

"So the Senate majority leader was prophesying by virtue of his office?"

"The Senate majority leader was the highest representative of America's highest representative body. By virtue of that office, he became the instrument to represent the nation, to speak on its behalf, to give voice to its response, and to deliver a prophetic word."

"So someone can prophesy without being a prophet. How does that happen?"

"The word is inspiration. When a prophet speaks, he does so under the inspiration of the Spirit. But prophets aren't the only ones who can speak or act under inspiration. The Bible itself is called the inspired Word of God because it was written by those under the inspiration of God's Spirit—not only by prophets. Even those who have no idea what they're doing or saying, even those who act and speak from other motives, as did Caiaphas, even a politician, well-meaning or not, may speak under the inspiration of God."

"Inspiration," I said. "Didn't he use that word in the speech?"

"He did. He said, 'I know that there is only the smallest measure of inspiration that can be taken from this devastation.'[3] He used it to introduce the prophecy."

"But he didn't intend to use it that way."

"Of course not. He used it to mean this is for the purpose of *inspiring you.* But the word means more than that, even in its most literal definition. *Inspiration*, from the Latin *inspiratio*, means to be *in-breathed* or *blown upon.*"

"Blown upon by...?"

"By the wind...by the breath...by the Spirit. That which is inspired is *God-breathed, Spirit-blown.* The word is defined as, '*a supernatural or divine influence upon the prophets, the apostles, and the sacred writers, or upon men, to enable them to communicate divine truth.*'"

"So the word has a double meaning."

"Yes, just as the prophetic words of Caiaphas had a double meaning. That which he intended to say and that which he didn't. What he didn't intend—that was the prophecy. So too with the Senate majority leader; the message he intended to say was '*the following words are going to inspire you.*'"

"And that's how most people would have understood it."

"Yes," said the prophet, "but then there was the message he *didn't* intend to say, which was this: *The following words do not come from my own initiative but are of divine origin, the same origin and influence by which the prophets spoke. What you're about to hear is a prophetic message.*"

"So even the word *inspiration* came forth by inspiration."

"Yes, that, as well as the prophetic address."

"What do you mean?" I asked.

"When you send a letter, you address it, you identify the one to whom it's being sent. So too biblical prophecies often contain prophetic addresses, introductions identifying the one or ones to whom it's being sent. It's there in Isaiah's prophecy: 'The Lord has sent forth a word to Jacob...Israel...Ephraim...Samaria...all the people.' So the prophecy is *addressed* to the people of Jacob, Israel, and Samaria. But now the same prophecy, the same message, is about to be given...prophetically sent, to a different people, and a different nation."

"America."

"Yes."

"So then it has to be *readdressed*. The prophetic address has to be changed."

"Exactly," he said. "And so it was. The majority leader omitted the original prophetic address that identified Israel as its recipient and put a different one in its place:

> "There is a passage in the Bible, from Isaiah that I think *speaks to all of us at times like this*.[4]

"Again, it's a message of two realms and double meaning. What the speaker meant to say was this: *'There's a passage in the Bible to bring comfort in times of crisis like this.'* And, of course, the Bible *is* filled with countless passages of comfort and encouragement..."

"But Isaiah 9:10 was not one of them."

"No," said the prophet, "not by a very long shot."

"So what he *didn't* mean to say..."

"What he *didn't* mean to say, but actually said, was this: *'There's a message from Scripture now given and speaking to America. The message is a prophetic word of warning, sent to a nation that once knew God, and appointed to be given and to speak at this particular time—the time when a nation is standing in danger of judgment.'* And then, after proclaiming the ancient vow, the Senate majority leader added on his own words:

> "The bricks have fallen down, but we will rebuild with dressed stone; the fig trees have been felled, but we will replace them with cedars. *That is what we will do*.[5]

"*That is what we will do*...just six words, but all that was needed to transform the vow. No longer was it an ancient vow of an ancient people. No longer was it merely a quotation. It was now the *vow itself*. It was now the vowing. The *we* of ancient Israel had transformed into the *we* of America. The act of national defiance was taking place not in the ancient capital of an ancient kingdom; it was now transpiring on Capitol Hill in Washington DC. The ancient judgment drama was now playing itself out on the floor of the United States Senate. And then the Senate majority leader brought it to its logical conclusion:

"That is what we will do. We will rebuild and we will recover.⁶

"It was the final restating of the vow. '*That is what we will do.*' In other words, 'America will do exactly as ancient Israel had done in its days of judgment.'"

"Which is…"

"The word *that*, as in '*That is what we will do,*' can only refer to the ancient vow. In other words, America would continue in its defiance of God, in its departure from His ways, in its refusing to hear His call to return—only it would do so all the more. America would follow the course of the ancient vow."

"So Isaiah 9:10 is now being transformed into national policy."

"You could say that."

"And what happened after the vow was spoken?" I asked.

"Everyone was in full agreement," he replied.

"They had no idea what it was they had just heard."

"No. They had no idea what had happened, that which had gone forth from Capitol Hill was the proclamation that identifies a nation in rebellion against God and the pronouncement of judgment upon that nation."

"And what happened after that?"

"What happened after that…After that, it would all come true. It was a prophecy. It foretold the nation's future course. '*That is what we will do.*' America would choose the same course as that of ancient Israel, enact the same strategy, and walk in the same footsteps. It was all prophesied on the very morning after 9/11."

"He spoke of the cutting down of the tree. Did he know there was an actual tree cut down by the calamity at Ground Zero and that it bore the same name as the fallen tree of Isaiah 9:10?"

"No. He had no idea. His version translated it as *fig tree.* Nevertheless, it was the biblical *shakam*, the fig-mulberry tree, the sycamore. And even if he *had* known what he was saying, what it all meant, he could have had no idea that it was actually being fulfilled.

When he proclaimed the prophecy on September 12, Ground Zero was still a disaster site and cut off from the public. And it was only in later days that the story of the Sycamore of Ground Zero would come out. And yet he spoke of it. Nor could he have known on September 12 that one day a crane would lower a twenty-ton Gazit Stone onto Ground Zero where the fallen bricks had laid. That would come true three years after he foretold it."

"And the cedar tree," I said. "There's no way he could have known that a tree matching the biblical Erez Tree would actually be planted in place of the fallen Sycamore."

"That too would only happen years later…and only because someone decided to donate that particular tree. He couldn't have had any idea, and yet he prophesied it, that the one would be planted in place of the other. It was all prophesied the day after 9/11. It was all there, and recorded in the Annals of Congress, for the whole nation to know. The nation would respond to its calamity just as ancient Israel had responded to its calamity. It would pursue a course of defiance on a path of judgment."

I was silent. The prophet paused before saying anything more, allowing me time to process what I was hearing before showing me something else.

"Come, Nouriel. I want you to see something." He led me to the other side of the Capitol and pointed to a nearby building.

"Do you know what that is?"

"I feel I should."

"What you're looking at is the Supreme Court—the highest court in the land. And yet there sits a much higher court than this by which nations are judged. According to biblical requirement, before a truth can be established or a judgment passed in a court of law, the matter must be confirmed by two witnesses:

"One witness shall not rise against a man concerning any iniquity or any sin that he commits; by the mouth of two or three witnesses the matter shall be established.[7]

"The principle of two witnesses applies first to the legal realm. But it can also be applied to the realm of nations. In the case of America, the Isaiah 9:10 connection would, likewise, be established by two witnesses."

"The Senate majority leader on the day after 9/11...he was the first witness."

"Correct...And the second witness?"

"The vice presidential candidate three years later on the anniversary of 9/11. Both would speak the same words."

"Correct. And both would bear witness of the joining of America to ancient Israel and of 9/11 to Isaiah 9:10—the one speaking of what would be and the other of what was...that the vow was being fulfilled."

"And neither of the two," I added, "had any idea what they were saying, or what the other was saying, or how their words were actually being fulfilled in reality."

"No," said the prophet, "which only further compounds the weight of their testimony."

"And it was all set in motion on the very day after 9/11...here...with a warning...and the pronouncement of judgment. The prophecy was proclaimed to the nation from Capitol Hill...and it would all come true."

———————◆◆◆———————

There was silence. The revelation of the Ninth Harbinger was finished...and I was still shaken. This obscure...mysterious prophecy...had actually been proclaimed from the seat of the American government, and the speaker linked it all to 9/11. That, together with everything else—all the connections, all the twists and quirks, the reenactments, the replaying, the ancient mystery manifesting in America—it left me shaken. I wanted to be silent, to try to take it all in. But I had the sense that if I didn't say something soon, he'd be gone, and it would be the end. It was the last Harbinger. So I broke the silence.

"I have a question."

"Yes."

"If America is following the same pattern as ancient Israel, witnessing the same signs, uttering the same words, reenacting the same acts, responding with the same response..."

"Yes...?"

"How can it escape suffering the same fate?"

He didn't answer. So again I spoke.

"And if the proclaiming of the vow was just the *first* stage of judgment for Israel, and not the last, then what about America? What does the future hold?"

Chapter 14

There Comes a Second

א ת

AGAIN THE PROPHET was silent, and he gazed out into the expanse of the Washington Mall, appearing to be preoccupied.

"This was the *last* Harbinger," I said, trying to get his attention. "What's next?"

"What's next?"

"What happens now?" I asked. "What does it all lead to?"

"The Harbingers are signs of what, Nouriel?"

"Of warning."

"And of what else?"

"The rejection of the warning."

"And what's the purpose of a warning?"

"To prevent something from happening...a threat, a danger."

"So what happens if a warning is given, if the alarms go off, and nobody listens?"

"Then it happens."

"So then it happens."

"But does it have to happen?" I asked.

"If the warning is rejected, then, yes, it has to happen."

"But people can change, and a nation can alter its course."

"Yes. That's the hope. That's the purpose of a warning. A changed course means a changed end. But an unchanged course means an unchanged end. Then it has to happen."

"As it did to ancient Israel?"

"Each case is unique. But the overall progression is the same."

"So if America's course doesn't change...then what? Another 9/11?"

"Another 9/11 could be…or a different 9/11. Or was 9/11 itself a harbinger?"

"And what does that mean?" I asked.

"The first Assyrian invasion of Israel was a calamity in and of itself. But at the same time, it was a harbinger of a still greater calamity to come, a warning of the nation's destruction. A calamity can also be a warning."

"But what would 9/11 be a harbinger of?"

"It was the day of falling symbols. But what is the fall of a symbol?" he asked.

"I have no idea," I replied.

"Is it not also the symbol of a fall?"

"I'm not getting it."

"But you will."

"So first the warning's given, and then a final calamity."

"More than one warning may be given," said the prophet. "If one alarm is ignored, then there comes a second."

"Then there *comes* a second, or there *may* come a second?"

"Then there *comes* a second."

"Then a second warning is coming?" I asked.

"A second warning," he said, "a second alarm…a second shaking."

"A second shaking of America?"

He turned his gaze so that he was now looking directly into my eyes as he gave his response.

"There comes a second," he said again.

Then he handed me a seal. It was the same one I had just given him back.

"The seal of the Ninth Harbinger? I just returned it to you."

"Yes," he replied.

Then he began descending the Capitol steps. I followed after him. But hearing my footsteps, he stopped and turned around. "No, Nouriel," he said. "That was the last Harbinger. Our time is finished."

He resumed his descent. I stayed where I was. But I shouted

after him as I had done before, only now with more urgency at the thought that it might be my last chance of getting an answer.

"So what do I do now?"

"About what?"

"About everything. About everything you've shown me…"

"You don't forget it."

"That's not enough. I need something specific. What do I do now…specifically?"

When he got to the bottom of the first set of steps he stopped, turned around, and responded. "Specifically?" he said.

"Yes, specifically," I replied.

"You go home. You go home…and you watch."

"And what am I watching for?"

"*There comes a second,*" he replied.

He descended the next set of stairs as I finished descending the first. Then, from the terrace in between the two staircases, I watched as he walked away from the Capitol and down the Washington Mall…until he disappeared from my sight.

◆◆◆

Ana waited for something more, for the account to continue. She was hoping it wasn't end of the story. But Nouriel was silent.

"So what did you do after he left?" she asked.

"I went home."

"And…?"

"I watched."

"For what exactly?"

"For what exactly I wasn't sure. I focused on the prophecy. I went back to the library and spent hours and hours searching…poring through the commentaries on Isaiah 9:10."

"And…?"

"I found a match—what the prophet said to me when he left and what the commentaries said about Isaiah 9:10…they matched."

"How?"

"In one of the commentaries I found this:

"Divine anger, *being a remedial force, will not cease until its purposes are wrought out*... Therefore, if...Israel *resisted one expression of the anger, another must be found*."[1]

"And that means what?" she asked.

"It means that there was a purpose behind that first calamity, that first invasion of the land by the Assyrians. Its purpose was *remedial*—to correct, to wake up the nation, to turn it back to God, a purpose of redemption."

"But you knew that already," she replied. "What did you get from the commentary that was different, or that matched what the prophet told you?"

"What it's saying is that those purposes won't stop until they're fulfilled. So if a nation rejects one expression of that purpose, *another must be found*. The force or purpose will manifest itself again in another form. That's what I found in the one commentary. And then, in a second commentary on Isaiah 9:10, I found this:

> "God's first acts of judgment did not result in the transformation or 'repentance'...of his people Israel. The purpose of God's initial disciplinary punishment was to restore his people, but the people stubbornly refused to turn to him.... Since the first act of discipline did not bring about a humble confession of sins, *a second punishment was necessary*.[2]

"The commentaries were consistent in linking Isaiah 9:10 with the same principle. And then, in another commentary, I found this:

> "As the first stage of the judgments has been followed by no true conversion to Jehovah, the Almighty Judge, *there comes a second*."[3]

"'*There comes a second*.' That's what the prophet kept saying to you the day you last saw him."

"He kept saying it because he knew it wasn't the end. Isaiah 9:10 is the beginning, the first link in a chain of progression. There's more to it. It leads to something else."

"So then if Isaiah 9:10 is joined to America with the Harbingers, it means that what happened on 9/11 isn't the end of the matter. Then it's not over; there's more to come."

"Yes. Then there comes a second."

"A second what...exactly?"

"A second warning...a sounding of the alarm...a second chastening...a second shaking."

"But what exactly? What form does it take?"

"The prophet spoke of the Harbingers as symbols. That was a clue. The World Trade Center was a symbol of America's global financial and economic power. So what would such a fall foreshadow?

"An economic...fall?"

"As in a financial and economic collapse."

"The collapse that began the *Great Recession*?"

"Yes."

"The collapse of the American and global economy is connected to 9/11?"

"Yes."

"But how?"

"It all goes back to the prophecy...everything—the collapse of Wall Street, the rise and fall of the credit market, the war in Iraq, the collapse of the housing market, the foreclosures, the defaults, the bankruptcies, the government takeovers—everything—politics, foreign policy, world history—everything that happened after. It all goes back to the prophecy and to the ancient mystery."

"That's a pretty big proposition," she said. "In fact, it's colossal."

"I realize that," he said.

"And nobody else realizes it? All the economists and experts and think tanks and intelligence agencies, they have no idea?"

"I don't know. I guess not."

"But how do *you* know?" she asked. "How did you put it all together?"

"I told you," he replied. "It wasn't me. It was what I was told."

"I understand that...with the Harbingers. But now you're talking about what happened *after* you were shown the Harbingers. So how did you come to know these things if the last time you saw the prophet was on Capitol Hill?"

"But it wasn't the last time."

"He reappeared?"

"When we parted that day on the Capitol steps, it was the first time he left me without a seal... or without a new seal. So I assumed there was nothing more to be revealed. I didn't think I'd ever see him again. Still, occasionally I'd walk alongside the Hudson to the place where we first met, in the hope that he'd reappear. But he never did. Several years passed, and just when I had given up any hope of seeing him again..."

"...he reappeared?"

"He reappeared."

"But the last time you saw him, he told you that his time with you was finished."

"It *was* finished. He appeared the first time to reveal the first part of the mystery. The first part was complete. But there was more."

"So he appeared again, but this time to reveal the second part of the mystery?"

"Because there comes a second."

Chapter 15

The Isaiah 9:10 Effect

את

A T THAT HE was quiet. She was quiet as well, thinking it right to give him a chance to rest from speaking but, at the same time, concerned that if she waited too long, he might not continue. Finally she broke the silence.

"You *are* planning to tell me the second part of the mystery," she asked.

"As long as you have the time," he replied.

"Forget time," she said. "I want to know the second part."

"I know how busy you are."

"Not any more, Nouriel."

"I just wanted to make sure."

"Wait. Before you continue...what if we go for a walk? I need to walk, if that's OK with you."

"It's fine."

They left the office, took an elevator down to the first floor, exited the building, and began walking down the street. They would walk down many streets that night, passing office buildings, stores, street vendors, apartment houses, and others also walking the city streets that night. But the two were largely oblivious to their surroundings, caught up in the ancient mystery and the words of the prophet.

"So when did you see him again?" she asked.

"I was working on a project that had me in Lower Manhattan for several weeks. During my free time, I'd go for walks around the area. One day, during one of those walks, I stopped in front of the New York Stock Exchange. I was staring at it, at the side with the columns, the famous side. I don't remember exactly what I was thinking when I heard the voice."

"The voice of the prophet..."

"It had been several years since I last heard it."

◆◆◆

"You didn't forget, did you?" he said.

I turned around. He hadn't changed...nor had his long dark coat. He looked the same as when I last saw him. "Forget what?" I asked.

"What you were shown."

"I recorded everything. But, no, I didn't forget."

"Good. And how have you been, Nouriel?" It was the first time he ever asked me that.

"OK, I guess," I replied. "And you? What have you been up to these past few years?"

"Watching," he answered.

"Watching."

"And now to begin the second part."

"The second part of..."

"The mystery. Are you ready to begin?"

"I don't think I've ever been ready."

"Then let's begin. What concerns us now is that which comes after...starting with the prophecy. What comes after Isaiah 9:10?"

"What do you mean?"

"What comes after Isaiah 9:10?"

"Isaiah 9:11."

"Not the number...the words."

"I can't remember...offhand."

"Isaiah 9:10:

> "The bricks have fallen,
> But we will rebuild with hewn stone;
> The sycamores have been cut down,
> But we will plant cedars in their place.[1]

"Now, Isaiah 9:11:

> "Therefore the LORD shall set up
> The adversaries of Rezin against him,
> And spur his enemies on.[2]

"So what's going on in Isaiah 9:11?" he asked.

"The nation's first shaking is followed by a second?"

"And why is that?"

"Because the nation didn't wake up or turn back after the first."

"Isaiah 9:10 is a vow of defiance. Isaiah 9:11 is a prophecy of future calamity. The two are connected. The one leads into the other. The first brings about the second."

"So the vow brings about the nation's future calamities?" I asked.

"The vow," he replied, "but not the vow alone. If it were only a vow and nothing more, it would have ended differently. It's what the nation did once the vow was made that determined its future."

"Which was?"

"It fulfilled the vow with quarried stones and sycamores. The nation embarked on a campaign to rebuild and fortify itself, to emerge stronger and greater than before... "

"So by executing the vow... the vow to defy the first calamity... the nation ends up ushering in the second."

"Or the second disaster is brought about by the very campaign to prevent it."

"But why?"

"What would happen, Nouriel, if a gardener tried to remove a weed from his garden by cutting off its leaves?" he asked.

"The leaves would grow back," I replied.

"And if he cut off its stem..."

"It would sprout another."

"His efforts would be doomed to fail. You can't solve a problem by dealing with its symptoms... its manifestations. You have to deal with the cause behind it. In the case of the gardener, the cause lies hidden beneath the surface, in the roots. So even if he solves one problem, another will reappear... and another... and another...until he finally deals with the underlying problem...the root."

"So, in other words, Israel's real problem was a spiritual one—its separation from God. Everything else was just a symptom, or manifestation, of the underlying problem. So the vow to rebuild is like a gardener attempting to remove a weed by cutting off its leaves."

"Exactly. The ultimate problem wasn't national security or defense or the Assyrians or even the attack. If a nation's underlying problem is spiritual, then all the political, economic, or military solutions will do nothing to remove it. Such things can only treat symptoms—the bricks and the sycamores. A spiritual problem can only be solved by a spiritual solution. Apart from that, every solution will end up producing another crisis."

"So the only solution is to return to God."

"But Israel would choose otherwise. The nation would harden itself, seeking to come back stronger without addressing its spiritual descent. And the strategy appeared to be working...for a time. The clearing away of the ruins, the construction, and the sight of a nation rebuilding itself created a sense of national resurgence. But it was all an illusion. The judgment hadn't been averted—only masked. The root problem was never addressed. They were moving farther and farther away from God. The resurgence was hollow. They had vowed to rebuild. But what they were building was a house of cards. And in time it would all collapse."

"And it all began with the vow."

"It was the vow that set it all in motion," he said. "The same spirit of defiance that led to the vow would eventually lead Israel to reassert itself, to flaunt its strength, and, through a series of strategic maneuvers, to challenge the Assyrian Empire. That challenge would lead to calamity. So it was the vow, and the spirit behind the vow, that triggered a chain of events that would ultimately bring about the nation's destruction."

"The Harbingers are manifestations of the vow," I said. "So is it inevitable that the Harbingers lead to..."

"Calamity? The Harbingers lead either to calamity or redemption.

If heeded, they lead to redemption; if not, then to calamity. Now…it's been years, Nouriel, but is it possible that you still have the last seal?"

I reached into my coat pocket and pulled it out.

◆◆◆

"The one he gave you at the Capitol?" Ana asked.

"Yes…with the image of the scroll on it…the seal of the Ninth Harbinger."

"But you gave up on seeing him again."

"That's right."

"So why did you still have it with you?"

"I didn't know I *did* have it until I reached into my pocket. For a time…after that last meeting, I made sure to keep it with me, as I did with every seal. But after giving up hope of seeing him again, I wasn't as careful to make sure. Still, it was there in the pocket of my coat…and that's what I just *happened* to be wearing that day."

"So you gave him the seal."

"And as he examined it, he began to speak."

◆◆◆

"If a nation rejects the call of God to return, and if the Harbingers aren't heeded, then comes a second stage. So we move now to the second stage, within which are contained four mysteries."

"Four mysteries…"

"Do you see this?" he asked as he pointed to the image on the seal…to what looked like a shadow around the scroll, a shadowy double image. It was faint, and nothing that would have struck me or anyone as noteworthy.

"It's significant?" I asked.

"It's a double image…a second image."

"A second image as in *there comes a second*?" I asked.

"As in *there comes a second,* yes. So what would it mean?"

"The prophecy has a second part, it leads to something else…to a second manifestation."

"The Isaiah 9:10 Effect."

"Which is what?"

"This:

> "*The attempt of a nation to defy the course of its judgment, apart from repentance, will, instead, set in motion a chain of events to bring about the very calamity it sought to avert.*"

"And this all has to do with America?" I asked.

"Seven years after 9/11," he said, "the American economy collapsed, triggering a global economic implosion. Behind it all, and all that followed, was something much deeper than economics."

"Behind the collapse of Wall Street and the American economy was...."

"Isaiah 9:10."

"How?"

"The explanations for an economic collapse are endless," he said. "No one factor stands alone. And one can go back in time as far as one chooses to search for causes. But according to the Isaiah 9:10 Effect, the second calamity must be effectively born out of the first...and out of the nation's response to that first calamity."

"So then the collapse of the economy and Wall Street would have to somehow go back to 9/11."

"And it all *does* go back to 9/11," he said. "The smoke was still hovering over Ground Zero when the ancient vow of defiance was proclaimed from Capitol Hill. In the days and years that followed, the nation would attempt to fulfill that vow. The rebuilding was never just about Ground Zero—but about rebuilding the entire nation. Remember what was proclaimed over the hewn stone:

> "It will forever remain a symbolic cornerstone for the *rebuilding* of New York *and the nation.*[3]

And when the ancient vow was proclaimed in its entirety, it happened in Washington DC, the nation's capital. In both cases, it clearly had to do with more than Ground Zero and New York.

It was about America as a nation. And it would be the nation as a whole that carried out the vow. Just as it happened in ancient Israel, it would happen in post-9/11 America—the vow would be turned into reality. Isaiah 9:10 would become the nation's foreign and domestic policy."

"How so?"

"What did *'We will rebuild'* mean for ancient Israel?" he asked.

"It meant they would repair the damage and rebuild their fallen buildings, towers, homes…"

"And their *walls*," he added. "They would rebuild their walls and fortify their defenses so as to become invulnerable to future attacks. In the same way, America, after 9/11, would embark on a campaign to rebuild its walls of protection, to strengthen and fortify its systems of defense. The campaign would mean the establishing of the Department of Homeland Security, the launching of a global war against terror, and two conventional wars abroad, one in Afghanistan and the other in Iraq. It was all a reaction to 9/11. America was doing exactly as ancient Israel had done in Isaiah 9:10—attempting to defy the first calamity. In fact, the speech that would launch the nation's War on Terror would contain the words, *'We will rebuild.'* America was waging war against 9/11, trying to reverse its consequences, overcome its impact, and nullify its danger. So in the years following the attack, American foreign and domestic policy was, in effect, a translation of the ancient vow."

"But was it wrong?" I asked. "What choice was there?"

"Is it wrong for a gardener to cut off the stem of a weed," he asked, "instead of dealing with its root? The issue was deeper. You can't solve a spiritual problem with a military or political solution. Apart from a return to God, the root issue remains untouched and will manifest again in a different form. It's in this that the Isaiah 9:10 Effect begins to operate. A nation's attempt at defying judgment apart from repentance ends up setting in motion a future calamity. In its campaign to strengthen itself, it ends up bringing about its own weakening."

"So, then, as America vowed to emerge stronger than before and wage war against 9/11, the Isaiah 9:10 Effect was set in motion."

"Yes. And each campaign born of that defiance would end up producing a backlash."

"How so?" I asked.

"The campaign to strengthen America's national security and defenses would require massive expenditures. The War on Terror, the military campaigns in Afghanistan and Iraq, would add multiplied billions of dollars to the federal budget. Funds and resources that otherwise would have been used to strengthen the American economy were now diverted and drained away from investment. The war in Iraq would impel a surging of oil prices, further draining the nation's gross domestic product. The massive amount of governmental spending in support of the nation's War on Terror would lead to the skyrocketing of the national debt, further draining its economy. And beyond the financial consequences, what America began in the wake of 9/11 would end up further dividing the nation."

"And it all would lead up to the economic collapse?"

"In part," he said. "And for all that, it would be yet another manifestation of the Isaiah 9:10 Effect that would bring about the collapse of the American and global economy. And this too was born out of the ruins of 9/11. The most critical effect of the calamity on the American and global economy would begin six days after the attack."

"As a response to the calamity?"

"Yes," he said, "as in the ancient vow. In January 2001, with the American economy beginning to slow down, the Federal Reserve began reducing the target interest rate, lowering it to 3.5 percent by the summer of that year. Then came 9/11. The first economic impact of the attack was the closing down of the New York Stock Exchange the same day. The market would remain closed for six days. When it reopened the following Monday, it would suffer the largest point crash in Wall Street history up to that time.[4] The attack had inflicted a damaging blow to an already fragile economy. In the days and months after September 11, there was a pervading fear that the calamity would cause the economy to hemorrhage. The repercussions of 9/11 and of the nation's response to it would continue to affect the economy long after those initial fears had vanished along with the ruins of Ground Zero, long after even what appeared to be an economic rebound. September 11 would not only continue to affect the American economy but would also alter it and, in so doing, change the global economy."

"So what happened six days after the attack?"

"The Isaiah 9:10 Effect begins with the nation's response to the first calamity."

"So the effect would begin with the proclaiming of the vow on Capitol Hill, the next day."

"Yes," said the prophet, "but those were words, '*We will rebuild.*' It would be the following Monday that those words would be translated into reality. It was the day that the Federal Reserve attempted to inject liquidity into the market in a campaign to avert economic disaster and ensure that America would indeed rebuild and recover."

"As ancient Israel had attempted to defy the consequences of its first calamity."

"Yes, except that the hewn stones of America's recovery were primarily economic. So on the first Monday after 9/11, the Federal Reserve slashed its target interest rate still further...as the first concrete act of the nation's rebuilding. The rate had already been lowered to 3.5 percent. But the extreme nature of 9/11 would now cause it to begin descending to extreme levels. That Monday morning of September 17, the Federal Reserve lowered the target interest rate by fifty basis points. Over the next three months it would be slashed several more times until hitting 1.75 percent on December 11, 2001.[5] September 11 would force the interest rate below the rate of inflation."

"Which is equivalent to creating free money."

"The Treasury would continue its extreme suppression of interest rates over an extended period of time. By June of 2003, the rate would reach 1 percent and would remain under 2 percent for several years. Only after that would it be adjusted upward. But the severe slashing and prolonged suppression of interest rates in reaction to

9/11 would set in motion a chain of events that would bring down the American and global economy."

"How...exactly?" I asked.

"The extreme rates would open up an era of easy money," he explained, "easy loans, easy borrowing, and easier mortgages. Easier mortgages would cause an already rising housing market to explode beyond all standard economic fundamentals, creating an unprecedented housing and building boom. The exploding housing market would lead homeowners to borrow and spend against the rising value of their homes. The phenomenon would create credit bubbles throughout the economy. This, in turn, would encourage massive inflows of capital from Asia to compound the problem. The stock market would surge along with the volume of monies borrowed and leveraged. And the effect would spread throughout the world. The post-9/11 slashing of interest rates would be copied by central banks across the globe, meaning that the same post-9/11 dynamics at work in America were now reproduced throughout the world—with similar consequences: credit bubbles, building and housing booms, and exploding markets."

"So what spread around the world throughout the global economy was, in a sense, the continuing effect of 9/11."

"And of the Isaiah 9:10 Effect."

"But was it wrong?" I asked.

"No more wrong than replacing fallen bricks with quarried stone or sycamores with cedar trees—if nothing more was involved. But there *was* something more involved, something *much* more involved. A nation was in spiritual decline and rapid departure from God. God was calling it back, allowing it to be shaken, to wake it up, to save it from judgment. But it chose instead not to turn back. And without turning back, all its efforts, all its campaigns become, in effect, acts of defiance, the undoing of symptoms, the silencing of alarms, with no resolution of the underlying problem."

"The foolish gardener."

"The remedies only masked the problem, just as happened with ancient Israel. The Assyrian invasion was followed by a campaign to rebuild what had been destroyed, fallen buildings, walls, towers, homes, a massive wave of construction throughout the land."

"Like a building boom," I said.

"Like a building boom. So too 9/11 not only resulted in the rebuilding of what had been destroyed but, beyond that, a massive wave of building throughout the nation, a building boom linked to the suppression of interest rates, linked to America's defiance of 9/11, linked to Isaiah 9:10 and to the words, '*We will rebuild.*'"

"And to the words proclaimed from Capitol Hill just days before the Treasury lowered the rate."

"Yes," said the prophet. "And since the economic boom was linked to Isaiah 9:10…the Isaiah 9:10 Effect…it ultimately had to collapse. *The attempt of a nation to defy the course of its judgment, apart from repentance, will, instead, set in motion a chain of events to bring about the very calamity it sought to avert.* The words of Isaiah 9:10 would lead Israel to its downfall, and all its rebuilding and all its prosperity would be destroyed. All the trappings of its national resurgence would then be exposed as having been hollow, empty, and deceptive from the start."

"A house of cards," I said.

"And so too in the case of America," he said. "The extreme and prolonged lowering of interest rates would sow the seeds of future disaster. The explosion in credit would lead to a massive explosion in debt. The increased liquidity would mask a multitude of economic dangers. The standard cautions and restraints involved in borrowing and loaning would be thrown away. Banks would make loans they never otherwise would have made, consumers would spend money they never otherwise would have spent, and people would buy houses they never otherwise could have afforded. Personal debt, government debt, and corporate debt all mushroomed. And with increased pressure to produce ever greater profits, investment and banking firms would become involved with increasingly risky transactions and practices."

"An economic house of cards."

"And just as Israel's resurgence was a house of cards," he said, "so too was America's post-9/11 resurgence. As long as credit continued to flow, the stock market to rise, and the housing market to boom, the illusion could be sustained. But if the housing market stopped booming, if the stock market began to falter, or if the flow of credit began to dry up, the illusion would collapse."

"And so it did."

"In September of 2008, the American financial system began to implode, triggering the greatest economic disaster since the Great Depression. The American-led global economic explosion turned into an American-led global economic implosion. The house of cards was collapsing and drawing the world into its fall. And so behind the entire global economic collapse…was Isaiah 9:10. It all began in the ruins of 9/11."

"Did anyone else see the connection between the economic implosion and 9/11?"

"In time it became clear to more and more analysts. One observer would put it this way:

> "We can trace the roots of the crisis back to the 9/11 terror attacks…[Greenspan] kept on cutting the interest rates after September 11th, pushing financial innovation.…After 9/11 American people were encouraged to spend, spend, spend in the spirit of patriotism, to help restart the flailing economy.…To fuel that spending, in the extraordinary political and psychological climate of that time, U.S. policy makers actively encouraged levels of borrowing and lending that would never otherwise have been allowed."[6]

"Isaiah 9:10 translated into modern economics."

"Exactly. And from another source:

> "The financial house of cards was slowly built following the 9/11 attacks. As the U.S. government tried to revive the economy by repeatedly dropping interest rates, families lunged at the opportunity to refinance their mortgages. Now, the collapse of the mortgage market is felt around the world."[7]

"'*Divine anger*,' I said, quoting what I had read, '*being a remedial force, will not cease until its purposes are wrought out....If one expression is resisted another must be found.*'"

"And where did you get that?" he asked.

"From a commentary on Isaiah 9:10."

"Very good, Nouriel. So you've been searching."

"America resisted one expression," I said, "so another was found."

"The warning was rejected," said the prophet. "The stem was cut. But the root brought forth another. So the economic crisis that engulfed America and the world was, in a sense, the continuation of 9/11."

"Or 9/11 manifesting in the form of an economic collapse."

"Or," he said, "that which first manifested as 9/11...now manifesting in an alternate form."

"There comes a second," I said.

"And notice, Nouriel, the dynamic keeps getting larger. It begins with the voicing of the ancient vow. Then it becomes a direction, then the policy of an entire nation, and then a collapse affecting the course of the entire world. The Harbingers draw in everything to themselves, from the Federal Reserve to the global economy..."

"They touch the entire world, and no one realizes that it's all part of the ancient mystery."

◆◆◆

He didn't say anything in response but reached into his coat, pulled out a seal, and handed it to me. I recognized it immediately. It was another of the Nine Harbingers.

"You realize you gave this one to me before as well?" I asked.

"I do."

"So you recycle?"

He didn't respond to that either, though I wasn't surprised.

"You're giving me the seal of the Sixth Harbinger."

"That's correct."

"The fallen Sycamore...the tree of Israel's judgment."

"And why am I giving it to you a second time?" he asked.

"Because it has something to do with the second shaking."

"It does," he said. "But also for another reason."

"What?"

"Within the Sycamore are two mysteries—one going back to the last days of ancient Israel, and the other going back to the first days…"

"The first days of ancient Israel?"

"The first days of America."

Chapter 16

The Uprooted

א ה

L OOK AT THE seal again," he said. "What do you see?"
"The Sycamore," I answered.

"Look deeper...not at the main image. Look to the left of it. What do you see?"

"Something that looks like some sort of wall."

"It *is* a wall."

"And...?"

He began walking, motioning to me to join him. We resumed the conversation, slowly making our way down the street, stopping several times along the way. "The Lord sent a word," he said, "through the prophet Ezekiel:

> "So I will break down the wall you have plastered with untempered mortar, and bring it down to the ground, so that its foundation will be uncovered; it will fall, and you shall be consumed in the midst of it. Then you shall know that I am the LORD.[1]

"*Its foundation will be uncovered.* What foundations do you think the prophecy is referring to, Nouriel?"

"The foundation of a wall, it would seem."

"A foundation is that upon which something stands or rests or is built. So a nation's foundation is that upon which it stands...or on which it was founded...or that in which it rests or places its trust. The nations of the ancient world trusted in their idols and gods. Modern nations trust in their powers, their militaries, their economies, their resources. But what it's saying here is that in the days of judgment a nation's foundations are laid bare. Its idols fall, and its powers fail.

It's one of the key signs of judgment—the laying bare of foundations. The Lord said this through the prophet Jeremiah:

> "Behold, what I have built
> I will break down,
> And what I have planted
> I will pluck up.[2]

"That which is built up is built up *from* the foundation. And that which is broken down is broken down *to* the foundation. So the Lord built up Israel as one builds a house and planted it as one plants a tree. But in the days of Israel's judgment, that which was built up would be broken down and that which was planted would be uprooted. Two images of national judgment—*the breaking down and the uprooting.*"

"Repeat that," I said.

"Repeat what?" he asked.

"Jeremiah's prophecy."

"*'Behold, what I have built I will break down.'*"

"*'The bricks have fallen,'*" I answered.

"*'And what I have planted I will pluck up.'*"

"*'The sycamores have been cut down,'*" I answered.

"Yes, Nouriel, it follows the same pattern."

"It's the same pattern and the same order as Isaiah 9:10. First comes the breaking down—the fallen bricks. Then comes the uprooting—the sycamore. And that's what actually happened on 9/11. First came the collapse of the buildings, and then the uprooting of the sycamore. The two images of national judgment—and in the same order."

"Yes," said the prophet, "and it goes deeper still. The World Trade Center was the towering symbol of American financial power, a power centuries in the making and long connected to the island of Manhattan, the island that long functioned as the focal point of the nation's economic and financial activity. As far back as the dawn of the seventeenth century, the island served as a trading outpost for the Dutch. Those first traders and settlers soon felt the need to protect themselves from Indians, pirates, and other perceived dangers. So they built a wall. Along the wall, merchants opened up shops and set up warehouses. In time, the wall became the center point of the island's trade and commerce. The Dutch would eventually lose the island to the British. The British would tear down the wall. Nevertheless, the road would continue to bear the name..."

"...of Wall Street!" I said.

"Correct."

"The street we're walking on right now—it's Wall Street."

"Yes. And it was from this street and from these beginnings that America's financial power would rise and this island become the nation's financial capital. Wall Street would become a channel for the pouring in and out of money to finance America's ascendancy to economic, commercial, and industrial superpower. Here, on this street, the nation's economic fortunes would rise and fall, and mostly rise. It would become the embodiment of American financial power. And in the twentieth century, as America emerged as the world's towering economic colossus, the power and reach of Wall Street would encircle the globe to become, in effect, the financial capital of the world."

"Pretty impressive," I said, "for a street that started out as a wall."

"Pretty impressive," he replied, "for any street. But how did it happen? What was it that transformed a road, just a few blocks long and that for decades was not even paved with cobblestones, into America's financial capital and laid the foundation for America's ascent as the world's preeminent financial superpower?"

"I think you're going to have to tell me."

"In March of 1792, a secret meeting took place at a Manhattan hotel. It involved twenty-four of the city's leading merchants. The purpose of the meeting was to bring order to the trading of stocks and bonds while protecting that trade from competition. Two months later on May 17, 1792, the merchants again gathered together, this time at 68 Wall Street to sign a document. The document would seal the goals set forth at the first meeting. It would be the founding of what would ultimately be known as the New York Stock Exchange. The document was called the *Buttonwood Agreement*.

The organization born of the agreement would be known as the *Buttonwood Association* and later as the *New York Stock and Exchange Board*, and finally as the *New York Stock Exchange*. It would become the nation's leading stock exchange and then, in the twentieth century, the world's. Thus on May 17, 1792, with the signing of the Buttonwood Agreement, the foundation was laid for the rise of America as the world's towering financial superpower. Do you know what *buttonwood* means, Nouriel?'

"No."

"It's the name of a tree," he said.

"What does a tree have to do with the founding of Wall Street?"

"The twenty-four merchants used to meet and carry on their transactions under a buttonwood tree that grew on Wall Street. It was under that tree that they signed the agreement that gave birth to the New York Stock Exchange. So both the founding document and the founding association were named after the tree under which it all began. Wall Street, as we know it, and American financial power, also as we know it, officially began under a buttonwood tree."

"May I ask a question?"

"Of course," he said.

"What kind of tree is a buttonwood?"

"You already know."

"What kind of tree?"

"A sycamore."

"A sycamore."

"*Buttonwood,*" he said, "is, in essence, just another way of saying *sycamore.*"

"So that document from which Wall Street began was, in essence, the *Sycamore Agreement.*"

"You could say that."

"And the New York Stock Exchange is, in essence, the *Sycamore Association.*"

"You could say that too," he replied.

"And all the consequences of American financial power—all of its world-changing repercussions—it all began under the branches of a sycamore tree."

"Yes," he said, "under the branches of a sycamore tree."

"And 9/11..."

"The World Trade Center was a towering symbol of what that power had become. But the sycamore was the symbol of its origin."

"The *foundation*," I said, "the foundation of a nation's power..."

"Which are exposed in the days of judgment. *'So I will break down the wall you have plastered with untempered mortar, and bring it down to the ground, so that its foundation will be uncovered.'*"

"And in that foundation was a sycamore...and growing in the shadow of the World Trade Center was the Sycamore of Ground Zero."

"Correct," he said. "And on 9/11, the fall of the one would cause the fall of the other."

"The fall of the symbol that stands for Wall Street."

"Yes," said the prophet, "just as 9/11 would strike a blow to Wall Street and the American economy—not only in those first days after the attack, but in the long-term economic damage it would inflict, culminating in the collapse of Wall Street seven years later."

"So the Sycamore wasn't only a warning of judgment; it was, at the same time, a specific foreshadow of economic collapse."

"The striking down of the sycamore tree is a biblical sign of judgment," he said. "But the same tree is also a symbol specific to American power."

"So then the uprooting of the sycamore would foreshadow..."

"Yes," he said, "it would foreshadow the uprooting of America's financial and economic power."

He walked ahead of me, then stopped when he saw that I wasn't keeping up.

"Come, Nouriel, I want to show you something." He led me to the end of Wall Street and into the courtyard of an old church, where there rested a strange-looking structure of bronze.

"Do you know what this is?" he asked.

"I have no idea."

"This was among the first of permanent memorials to commemorate 9/11. It was unveiled on September 11, 2005. Its creator intended it to memorialize one of the details of the tragedy in which many found a measure of inspiration."

"But it meant more than he intended it to mean?" I asked.

"Yes," he replied. "And do you know what it is?"

"It looks like some sort of root system."

"It *is* a root system. It's the root system of a particular tree...a sycamore."

"A particular sycamore tree?"

"Yes, it's the root system of the Sycamore of Ground Zero."

"How?"

"Its creator fashioned it according to the roots of the fallen tree. He intended it to be a symbol of hope."

"But a fallen sycamore is not a symbol of hope," I said, "It's a sign of judgment..."

"And a sign of uprooting," he added. "They placed it here at the end of Wall Street—the same street symbolized by the sycamore...now bearing the image of a sycamore uprooted."

"The foundation," I said, "the foundation of America's financial power. It's the exposing of the foundation."

"And a message," he replied, "a message from the prophets:

"Behold, what I have built
I will break down,
And what I have planted
I will pluck up."[3]

"So what does it mean?" I asked. "What does it mean specifically for America?"

"If a living sycamore signifies the rise of America as the world's preeminent financial power, what then does an uprooted sycamore signify?"

"Its fall," I answered. "It would have to signify its fall."

"God had allowed America's power to be planted here, to take root, to grow, and to branch out over the world. The nation would rise to unprecedented heights of global power and economic prosperity. But in its departure and its rejection of His ways, a sign was given. If now it refused to turn back, the blessings and prosperity symbolized by the sycamore would be removed—that which had been built up would be broken down, and that which had been planted would be uprooted."

◆◆◆

After a slight pause, he asked me for the seal. And, after placing it in his hand, I received another. "Do you remember this one too?" he asked as I looked it over.

"Of course. It's the Erez Tree."

"The Seventh Harbinger."

"But now you want me to see something else?" I asked.

"What do you see...in the background...around the tree?"

"Blades of grass."

"Look more carefully."

"Grain...stalks of wheat."

"How many?" he asked. "How many stalks?"

"Six," I answered. "Three on each side of the tree."

"Six stalks of wheat," he said, "and a seventh you don't see."

"How could there be a seventh, if I can't see it?"

"It's there," he said. "It's there in its absence."

"It's there in its absence...another mystery?"

"This next seal, Nouriel, is going to open up a whole other realm of mystery."

"And it has to do with the second shaking?" I asked.

"With the second...and with the first...and with that which joins the two together."

"As in the Isaiah 9:10 Effect?"

"Yes, but in this mystery the connections are even more beyond the realm of the natural."

"They're supernatural?"

"You could say that."

"And they connect 9/11 to the economic collapse?"

"Not only do they connect them...*they determined them*...down to the time each would take place."

"An ancient mystery?"

"Yes, an ancient mystery upon which the global economy and every transaction within it was determined, a mystery that begins more than three thousand years ago in the sands of a Middle Eastern desert."

Chapter 17

The Mystery of the Shemitah

א ה

A ND THEN HE left."

"So what happened?"

"I tried to figure out the mystery on the seal...the six stalks of wheat...and, in some way, a seventh...but not there...absent. Six of one kind and a seventh of another. It turns out, it's a biblical pattern—the days of the week, six days of one kind and a seventh day, the sabbath, different from the rest."

"But what do the days of the week have to do with wheat?" she asked.

"I had no idea. But that's all I could figure out."

"And then he reappeared...?"

"Several weeks later. I was driving home from a conference out of state, through the countryside. It was a rolling landscape with fields of grain on both sides of the road. On my left, the grain sloped upward to a distant crest. The wind was beating against the stalks, making waves throughout the field. I couldn't help looking at it while trying to keep my eyes on the road—a dance of wind, wheat, sunlight, and shadow. Then I noticed something out of place. At first I thought it was a scarecrow, it was the only thing I could think of...the figure of a man standing on the top of the crest."

"With a long dark coat?"

"It was him. Not that I could be sure from so far away, but I just knew it. So I pulled over to the side of the road, got out, and made my way through the field up to the crest."

◆◆◆

"Nouriel!" he said, greeting me as I approached. "What brings you to these parts?"

"Ah…of course…what would bring me to these parts?" I replied. "And would it do any good if I asked you what you're doing standing in the middle of a wheat field?"

"I can tell you I'm not here for the farm work."

"I knew it wouldn't do any good to ask," I replied.

"I'm here for the same reason you are."

I gazed out at the surroundings. The crest wasn't actually part of the field. The wheat stopped just short of reaching it. And we were surrounded not by one field but several in every direction, each one rolling away from us and up into the distant hills.

"So," he said, breaking the silence, "have you figured out the mystery of the seal?"

"Something to do with the days of the week."

"Why do you say that?" he asked.

"There were six stalks of wheat, and a seventh one I only know about because you told me. The six were visible; the seventh was not. A pattern of six and seven…the same pattern of the biblical week."

"You didn't get it," he said, "but you were on the right track."

"How so?"

"The pattern is correct, six of one kind and then a seventh. And each stalk of wheat represents a measure of time. You got that right. But it's not a pattern of days."

"Then of what?"

"The same pattern, given to Israel to mark their days, was also given for their years. For six years, they were to labor, sowing and reaping their fields, pruning their vines, gathering in their harvests. But in the seventh year, they would rest. It would be the Sabbath Year. The law of the seventh year came to them in the deserts of Sinai through Moses. Thus they were commanded:

"When you come into the land which I give you, then the land shall keep a sabbath to the LORD. Six years you shall sow your field, and six years you shall prune your vineyard, and gather its fruit; but in the seventh year there shall be a sabbath of solemn rest for the land, a sabbath to the LORD."[1]

"Then each stalk represents a year," I said. "Each stalk represents a harvest."

"Correct. And the missing stalk?"

"The missing stalk would stand for the seventh year. It's not there because the seventh year is the Sabbath Year. So there's no harvest."

"Well done," he said. "The seventh year was given a name. It was called the *Shemitah*. The word *Shemitah* means, *the release, the remission, the letting rest*. In the year of the Shemitah, all laboring over the land was to come to a rest. There was to be no plowing, no sowing, no pruning, no reaping, no harvesting. The fruits of the harvest would be abandoned...let go:

"What grows of its own accord of your harvest you shall not reap, nor gather the grapes of your untended vine, for it is a year of rest for the land.[2]

"Look over there, Nouriel. What do you see?"

"A field with no harvest," I answered.

"Only the remains of a past harvest. It's fallow ground. The land is resting. In the year of the Shemitah, all the fields of Israel became like that, fallow and resting."

"But how did they live without a harvest?"

"They would eat whatever grew of itself:

"Six years you shall sow your land and gather in its produce, but the seventh year you shall let it rest and lie fallow, that the poor of your people may eat.[3]

"In the seventh year, each landowner was required to open up his land to those in need. The poor would share equally in the fruit of the rich. The land's produce would become, in a very real sense, the possession of all."

The wind was now beginning to pick up in speed and strength, its gusts beating down all the more intensely on the stalks of wheat. The resulting waves were now more rapid and dramatic than before. The prophet paused for a few moments as I took it all in…then continued.

"But the Shemitah," he said, "touched not only the fields but also the people. The last remission took place in an entirely other realm:

> "At the end of every seven years you shall grant a release of debts. And this is the form of the release: Every creditor who has lent anything to his neighbor shall release it; he shall not require it of his neighbor or his brother, because it is called the LORD's release [*Shemitah*].[4]

"Thus, the last *letting go* of the Shemitah would touch the economic realm and transform it. So in the seventh year, all debts were canceled. Everyone who had made a loan had to annul it. Those in debt were released. Anything still owed was forgiven. All credit was nullified, all debt was wiped away."

"And all this took place at the *end* of the seventh year?" I asked.

"Yes, at the very end on one specific day—the twenty-ninth day of the Hebrew month of Elul, the last day of the civil year, the very end of the seventh year. So the twenty-ninth of Elul was the climax, the focal point, and the finale of the Shemitah—the day when the nation's financial accounts were nullified."

"But wouldn't the canceling of all debt and the nullifying of all credit cause economic chaos?"

"It could," he said. "Most economies are dependent on some sort of system of credit and loans. So the economic repercussions of such a sweeping change would be immense, so immense that, over the centuries, the rabbis would seek ways to get around these requirements in the fear that keeping them would cause economic disaster."

"But it was supposed to be a blessing," I replied, "a sabbath."

"Yes, a year of release and freedom, a year of rest from one's labors and of drawing near to God. And yet still, in outward form, it could resemble an economic collapse."

"But if the Shemitah Year was meant to be a blessing, what does it have to do with judgment—or Isaiah 9:10 or America?"

"The Shemitah *would* have been a blessing had Israel observed it and not rebelled against God. But Israel did rebel and didn't keep the Sabbath Year. And the breaking of the Sabbath Year became the sign of a nation that had ruled God out of its life. The nation had no more time for Him. The people were now serving idols. Their Sabbath Years would be filled, not with peace, but with the restless pursuit of increase and gain. The breaking of the Shemitah was the sign that the nation had driven God out of its fields, out of its labors, its government, its culture, its homes, its life. The Shemitah *was* meant to be a blessing, but in its breaking, its blessing turns into a curse."

"And what does that mean?" I asked.

"The Shemitah would still come," said the prophet, "but not by choice—but by judgment. Foreign armies would overrun the land, destroy the cities, ravage the fields, and take the people captive into exile. And the land would rest. The fields would become fallow. The buying and selling of its produce and the flow of commerce would come to a standstill. Private ownership would become virtually meaningless. And every debt, credit, and loan would, in an instant, be wiped away. One way or another, the Shemitah would come."

"Does the Bible connect the Shemitah to judgment...explicitly?"

"Yes," he answered. "The connection was foretold from the beginning, from Mt. Sinai:

> "Your land shall be desolate and your cities waste. Then the land shall enjoy its sabbaths as long as it lies desolate and you are in your enemies' land; then the land shall rest and enjoy its sabbaths. As long as it lies desolate it shall rest—for the time it did not rest on your sabbaths when you dwelt in it.[5]

"And it would all be fulfilled centuries later when the armies of Babylon invaded and ravaged the land and took multitudes into captivity. The people would remain in exile for seventy years. Why seventy? The answer was hidden in the mystery of the Shemitah."

"Seventy was the number of Sabbath Years not kept?"

"Correct."

"But now, with the land lying still for seventy years, the law of the Shemitah would be fulfilled, even if not by choice."

"Correct again."

"It's ironic. In the pursuit of prosperity the people drove God and the Shemitah out of the land. But now it was the Shemitah that drove the people out of the land...and their prosperity...nullifying all their gains and increase."

"And it was the Shemitah," he said, "in which was hidden the mystery of the timing."

"The timing?"

"The timing of their judgment—seventy years for seventy Shemitahs."

"So the Shemitah is meant to be a blessing, but for the nation that once knew God but has driven Him from its life, the Shemitah becomes a sign of judgment."

"Correct," he said. "So now let's piece the mystery together. In order to do that, we must first identify the pieces. Record this."

"I've recorded everything," I replied. "The machine's on."

"I don't mean that. You have your notepad?"

"Yes."

"And a pen?"

"Yes."

"You're a writer, Nouriel...write."

So I jotted down the next part in shorthand as he dictated:

> The effect and repercussions of the Shemitah extend into the
> financial realm, the economic realm, and the realms of labor,
> employment, production, consumption, and trade.

Over the course of the seventh year:

The nation's production is severely decreased as its fields and vineyards lay fallow.

The nation's labor is greatly reduced or comes to a cessation.

Its fields become, in part, the possession of all.

The buying and selling of the land's produce are restricted.

The fruits of labor are abandoned.

Credit is canceled and debt is wiped away.

For the nation that attempts to rule God out of its existence, the Shemitah changes from a vessel of blessing to a vessel of judgment—the judgment of a nation's prosperity.

"Did you get all that?" he asked.

"Yes. But what does it have to do with America? America has never had a Sabbath Year."

"That's correct. It was only commanded for one nation. But the issue here isn't the literal observance of the Shemitah or any requirement to keep it."

"Then what *is* the issue here?" I asked.

"The issue here," he replied, "is its dynamic, its effect, and its consequence."

"And what does that mean?"

"The issue is the Shemitah *as a sign*."

"The Shemitah as a *sign*…?"

"The sign of the Shemitah, given to a nation that has driven God out of its life and replaced Him with idols and the pursuit of gain. The issue is the Shemitah as a sign of judgment, the sign that specifically touches a nation's financial and economic realms."

"I still don't see how it connects with America."

"Behind the collapse of Wall Street and the implosion of the American and world economy, behind all of it lies the mystery of the Shemitah."

"Tell me."

"The economic collapse of 2008 was set off by a series of trigger events in early September. At that time, about half of the American mortgage market was owned or backed up by two corporations: the Federal National Mortgage Association and the Federal Home Loan Mortgage Corporation."

"Fannie Mae and Freddie Mac."

"That's right," he said, "and by early September, both of them, along with the mortgage and housing markets, were teetering on the edge of collapse. On September 7, in one of the most dramatic economic interventions since the Great Depression, the federal government seized control of both corporations, placing them under government conservatorship."

"In effect, nationalizing them."

"Their seizure caused global alarm. And then, just as the mortgage market was reeling from their collapse, an even more economically cataclysmic collapse was about to take place."

"The fall of Lehman Brothers."

"At the start of the twenty-first century, Lehman Brothers stood at the pinnacle of the world's leading financial firms. But when the subprime mortgage market began to disintegrate, Lehman's standing and assets began to collapse. When the news spread that a deal to rescue the ailing firm had fallen through, its shares plunged along with the stock market. The following day Lehman Brothers announced a loss of nearly four billion dollars. The day after that, the firm's stock plunged another 40 percent, and news spread that it was seeking a corporate buyer. In the following days, a flurry of emergency meetings took place between the Federal Reserve and the leaders of Wall Street in a frantic effort to prevent Lehman's end. But the effort failed, and on Monday morning, September 15, 2008, one week after the first collapse, came the second, and this time with no safety net to break the fall. Lehman Brothers filed for bankruptcy—the largest bankruptcy in American history up to that date. It would be called the collapse *heard around the world*. The fall of Lehman Brothers would, in turn, trigger the collapse of Wall Street and the global financial implosion."

"The worst economic crisis since the Great Depression," I said. "But what does it have to do with the mystery of the Shemitah?"

"In the days of the prophet Jeremiah, with Jerusalem lying in ruins and the people taken away in captivity, the key that held the timing of the nation's judgment was hidden in the mystery of the Shemitah."

"So there's something in the timing of the economic collapse that's significant?"

"The collapse of Lehman Brothers and the American economy took place over the course of one week. It was the anniversary week of another American calamity..."

"9/11."

"Yes, 9/11," he said. "The collapse of Fannie Mae and Freddie Mac happened on September 7. The collapse of Lehman Brothers began two days later on September 9 when it lost 45 percent of its value. It was on September 10 that it announced its loss of almost four billion dollars. The following day its stock took a second precipitous plunge."

"September 11."

"It was that second collapse on September 11 that Lehman's death knell sounded throughout Wall Street and Washington DC. It was then that the Federal Reserve set in motion a series of actions and emergency meetings that would end in the fall of Lehman Brothers, triggering the implosion of the American and global economy. It was also on that September 11 that a second fall reached its critical mass and a second alarm was sounded as the chief executive of AIG alerted the Federal Reserve of New York that his firm was, likewise, in critical danger of collapsing. Two alarms of the coming collapse, both sounding on September 11. So as the nation was commemorating the calamity of 9/11, a second calamity, one that would ravage the economic realm, was just beginning."

"And the time separating the two events..."

"Seven years," said the prophet. "There were seven years between the two."

"Seven years—the biblical period of time that concerns a nation's *financial* and *economic* realms."

"Yes," he replied, "and that concerns the judgment of those two realms. Seven years between the first and second shaking. And what happens, Nouriel, at the end of seven years?"

"At the end of the seven years comes the remission."

"'At the end of every seven years, you will have a release, a remission, a canceling of debts.' So it was a remission of what exactly?" he asked.

"Of credit and debt," I answered.

"And what did all these collapses have to do with?"

"Credit and debt," I replied.

"So not only did the collapse of 2008 take place at the seven-year mark from 9/11, but it specifically concerned the principle of the Shemitah. The collapse of Fannie Mae, Freddie Mac, and Lehman Brothers all concerned the issue of credit and debt. In the case of the first two, the government intervened. It was a bailout. The two corporations were relieved of their debts of over five trillion dollars."

"A remission of debt."

"The remission of debt," said the prophet, "whether temporary or permanent, a form of Shemitah."

"And in the case of Lehman Brothers...?"

"In the case of Lehman Brothers, the remission took on a different form. The government refused a bailout and the corporation went bankrupt. And by declaring bankruptcy..."

"Its debts were wiped away and its loans were canceled."

"Another form of Shemitah," he said, "another remission of debt."

"So the American and global financial collapse was triggered by the dynamic of the Shemitah..."

"Yes, and not only triggered by it."

"What do you mean?" I asked.

"Stock markets are built on investment. Money is given on the assumption that the investment will generate a return. In that sense it follows the outward form of credit and debt. Beyond this, the investments come not only from individuals but also from banking institutions, the funds of which represent loans, credit, and debt."

"But in the year of the Shemitah credit and debt are nullified."

"Exactly. The fall of Lehman Brothers set off an avalanche of financial collapses from Wall Street to Asia. It would continue to cause the convulsion of stock markets around the world for several months, plunging them to ever-new lows. Massive fortunes were wiped out overnight. The crashing of stock markets across the world meant that the funds invested had vanished and would not be paid back, at least not for the foreseeable future. Both credit and debt, trillions of dollars worth of credit and debt, had, in effect, been canceled. *'Every creditor who has made a loan to his neighbor will let it go, will cancel it'*...a Shemitah."

"How far back did it go," I asked, "the cancellation of debt in the Shemitah?"

"Back to the end of the last Shemitah," he replied, "to the last remission of debt."

"So the Shemitah would wipe away all the debts of the previous seven years?"

"Yes."

"And when the stock market crashed in September 2008, how much was wiped away?"

"All the gains of the past seven years, and then some."

"And it touched the entire world."

"It touched the entire global economy in the form of collapsing markets, vanishing investments, government bailouts, corporate and personal bankruptcies, and foreclosures...each of which was, in effect, a financial nullification."

"So, in each case, whether by bankruptcy, by aid, or by vanishing accounts, the burden was remitted...released...each becomes a form of Shemitah."

"Not only each," he said, "but all...the whole. The global economic collapse was, itself, one colossal Shemitah...made up of countless smaller ones."

"How far does the cycle go," I asked, "every seventh year in the past...and into the future?"

"The subject is for another time," he said. "The point now is the Shemitah as a *sign* of judgment."

"You spoke of a specific day when financial accounts had to be wiped clean, when credit and debt had to be nullified."

"The twenty-ninth day of Elul, 'the end of every seven years,' the Shemitah's final and climactic day, when all remaining loans, credits, and debts had to be nullified."

"So does the twenty-ninth of Elul have a part in the mystery?" I asked.

"With the fall of Lehman Brothers, the stock market would plunge more than 499 points. Over the next several weeks, the world's financial markets reeled wildly from the impact. In response, the United States Congress worked frantically to come up with a plan to reverse the implosion. The result was a bill proposing the largest government bailout in American history. In a surprise turn of events that shocked most observers, the bill was defeated. That morning, September 29, the New York Stock Exchange began its session with what many saw as an omen—the opening bell wouldn't sound. When news reached the stock market that the rescue plan had been defeated, Wall Street collapsed. In a single day it plunged more than seven hundred points. It was the crowning day in the first stage of the global collapse and, in terms of point loss, the worst day in the history of Wall Street. One financial analyst would sum up what happened on September 29 this way:

> "It was this event more than anything else that shattered market confidence. Over the next two weeks, the Dow fell close to 2,700 points, a decline of almost 25 percent...the damage had been done.[6]

"It was the climactic moment of the global implosion and the greatest single-day stock market crash in Wall Street history. Why did it happen?" he asked. "Why did it happen just when it did?"

I didn't answer. He paused before revealing the answer.

"The greatest single-day stock market crash in Wall Street history took place *on the twenty-ninth day of Elul*—the critical and crowning day of the Hebrew Shemitah."

"My God!" I exclaimed. It was the only thing that could've come out of my mouth at that moment.

"The day when financial accounts must be wiped away," he said.

"When credit and debt are nullified...and it all happened on the *exact* biblical day on which it was ordained to happen."

"On the exact biblical day specifically ordained to touch a nation's financial realm."

"And the timing...you said that the Shemitah holds the key to the mystery to the timing of the judgment."

◆◆◆

"Did you verify it," Ana interjected, "everything the prophet told you...the facts?" There was now an unsteadiness in her voice.

"I did," he replied.

"And it was all true?" she asked.

"It was all true."

"It's mind-boggling," she said. "The biggest crash in Wall Street history and the collapse of the global economy—all the manifestation of an ancient mystery. It's mind-boggling."

"I told you it would be."

"That you did."

"And there's more."

"Go on," she said.

◆◆◆

The prophet spoke of the number seven. "The Shemitah," he said, "revolves around the number seven—it's the *seventh* year. It begins and ends in the month of Tishri, the *seventh* month of the biblical year. It's a mystery of sevens. So could there be a mark left by the Shemitah...a sign of the mystery in the number seven?"

"I'm not getting it," I replied.

"The greatest stock market point crash in Wall Street history took place on the last and crowning day of the Shemitah. That evening, as the sun went down, it was the beginning of Tishri, the *seventh* month of the Hebrew year. What triggered the crash was the rejection of the largest government bailout in American history...a sum of..."

"...*seven* hundred billion dollars," I said.

"And how much of the stock market was wiped away that day?"

"Tell me."

"That which was wiped away added up to 7 percent. How many points did that 7 percent amount to? How many points were wiped away in that largest crash in Wall Street history?"

"I don't know," I replied.

"*Seven* hundred *seventy-seven* points were wiped away that day."[7]

"*Seven, seven, seven.*"

"On the final day of the seventh year.

"Do you realize," I asked, "how many things would have to be in place for that all to happen...to come out like that? All of Wall Street, the entire American economy, the entire world economy, every transaction, every stock bought and sold, everything...everything had to be in its exact position for it all to happen exactly as it did, at the exact time, and to that exact number. Who could have orchestrated all that?"

"God," he replied.

"I guess He's the only one who could have."

"Everything I've told you thus far, Nouriel, concerns the *end* of the Sabbath Year. But what about the *beginning*? Did anything happen to signal the beginning of the Shemitah?"

"Good question," I said. It was a rare opportunity to say such a thing to the prophet.

"The years leading up to the Shemitah were fat and prosperous. Buying, spending, investing, the stock market, the housing market, the credit markets—everything was booming. But as the Shemitah Year drew closer, more and more signs of economic danger began to surface. The rate of loan failures and housing foreclosures began to rise. The financial institutions backing up those loans and mortgages now found themselves in crisis. But the first definitive sign of what was yet to come took place a year before the global economic collapse. It happened in Britain, but as a repercussion of the failing American housing and credit market. In early September 2007, Northern Rock, Britain's fifth largest mortgage lender, collapsed. It was the first British institution to suffer a bank run in over a century. By the end of the crisis, Northern Rock would be nationalized."

"The remission of debt."

"It was the first such collapse in the growing credit crisis and a foreshadow of the failures, the collapses, and the interventions that would soon overtake the American and global economy."

"A first Shemitah."

"The fall of Northern Rock happened on September 13, 2007. September 13, 2007, on the Hebrew calendar, was the first day of the month of Tishri. The first day of Tishri is the day that *begins the Shemitah Year.* So the first major sign of the Shemitah took place on the exact day on which the Shemitah begins."

"So then, the day of Northern Rock's fall to the day of the greatest stock market crash in history should mark the beginning and end of the biblical Shemitah."

"And so it does," said the prophet."

"The exact beginning and end?"

"The exact beginning and end."

"And what happened in between?"

"In less than a month from the start of the Shemitah, the stock market, which, for the previous several years, had been rising, reverses its momentum. By early October, its long ascent comes to an end. It begins to fall. As the Shemitah year progresses, the stock market continues its descent, a slow motion crash. Billions and billions of dollars are wiped away."

"The remission of credit and debt."

"With the tightening of credit markets and the plunging of housing prices, increasing numbers of homeowners find themselves unable to make their mortgage payments. More and more begin defaulting on their mortgages, entering foreclosure."

"The cancellation of loans, another wiping away of credit and debt."

"And as they default, the firms standing behind those mortgages now find themselves absorbing greater and greater losses."

"Every creditor must release his debt."

"And so the economy continues to deteriorate as the absorbing of losses sets off still more crises. Shock waves reverberate throughout the financial world as some of the nation's most powerful lending institutions begin to fail. Some are bailed out or bought out through government intervention; others go bankrupt. Each failure, each remission, each Shemitah triggers the next and the next as the global economy continues disintegrating. Then, in late August, early September, as the year of Shemitah enters its last and climactic phase, so too does the financial crisis."

"With the collapse of Fannie Mae and Freddie Mac."

"Yes," he said, "and then of Lehman Brothers, and then of the global economy—everything reaching the climax on September 29, 2008, the last and climactic day of the Shemitah."

"Everything following the ancient pattern."

"Speaking of the ancient pattern, Nouriel, read back to me what you took down."

So I took out my notepad and began reading back the words of his dictation:

> *The effect and repercussions of the Shemitah extend into the financial realm, the economic realm, and the realms of labor, employment, production, consumption, and trade.*

"Thus," said the prophet, "the global crisis began in the financial realm but didn't stop there. Before long virtually every economic indicator and every major sector of the economy was affected. The crisis quickly spread into the realms of labor, commerce, production, and consumption. Continue."

> *Over the course of the seventh year, the nation's production is severely decreased as its fields and vineyards lay fallow.*

"So the crisis," he said, "causes industrial production to decline and, in some cases, to cease altogether as demand dries up. Corporations downsize, factories cut back on output, businesses close their doors."

> *The nation's labor is greatly reduced or comes to a cessation.*

"So the crisis batters the labor force, workers are laid off, unemployment skyrockets."

Its fields become, in part, the possession of all.

"So private corporations are increasingly bought out, bailed out, and nationalized, or else become increasingly subject to the public realm."

The buying and selling of the land's produce are restricted.

"So commerce and consumption suffer a massive decline. Consumers cut back on spending and sellers grow more desperate to find ways of reviving their sales."

The fruits of labor are abandoned.

"So merchandise sits untouched in stores and piles up in warehouses. The nations that rely most heavily on export trade now suffer extensive economic damage."

Credit is canceled and debt is wiped away.

"And so," he said, "the entire global collapse is a manifestation of the ancient mystery of the Shemitah."

"I have a question."

"Ask it."

"The stock market crash happened on the twenty-ninth of Elul, the last day of the seventh year. So that day was the *end* of a cycle of seven Hebrew years."

"Correct," he said.

"So then there has to be another part to the mystery. That which takes place on the twenty-ninth of Elul would be the *conclusion* of something that began seven years earlier."

"And...?"

"And so there should be something that took place seven years before the crash, something connected to it…something that led up to it…something that inaugurated the seven-year cycle."

"So, Nouriel, how would you find out if such a thing exists?"

"You'd have to count back seven years from the crash."

"Which would bring us to what?"

"The year 2001…to September…of 2001…the month of…"

"The month of 9/11," he said, finishing my thought.

"So then the seven-year cycle that reaches its conclusion in the global collapse would have had to have begun somewhere around the time of 9/11. It would go along with the Isaiah 9:10 Effect. It was 9/11 and the nation's response to 9/11 that led to the economic collapse seven years later."

"Good, Nouriel…but you were looking for an event of the Shemitah. It would have to be a major event transpiring in the *economic* realm."

"And…was there such an event?" I asked.

"There was," he replied.

"What was it?"

"It happened on Monday, September 17, 2001. It took place in the economic realm, and it would match…and would foreshadow what would happen seven years later."

"And it was…"

"It was the greatest stock market point crash in Wall Street history up to that day. The record would remain intact for seven years, seven years until the crash of 2008.[8] Take note, Nouriel, of what we have."

"What do we have?" I asked.

"A seven-year period that begins with a stock market crash and ends with a second stock market crash. We have a seven-year period framed by the two greatest stock market crashes in Wall Street history up to that time."

"A seven-year cycle beginning and concluding with two massive remissions of credit and debt."

"Which is what?"

"The Shemitah," I answered.

"Correct."

"It happens at the same time as the first and second shaking."

"And the mystery goes deeper still," he said. "What do you think it was, Nouriel, that caused the stock market crash of September 17, 2001?"

"What?" I asked.

"It was 9/11. It was 9/11 that caused the New York Stock Exchange to close down for six days and then, when it reopened the following Monday, to suffer the greatest loss in its history up to that day. The crash of September 17, 2001, was the aftershock of 9/11..."

"Just as the crash of 2008 was also the aftershock of 9/11...the extended aftershock...the Isaiah 9:10 Effect. So each one was an aftershock of 9/11—two shakings—and *'there comes a second.'*"

"And the two events were inextricably bound together, seven years apart. This too goes deeper still. The biblical year isn't based on the Western Gregorian calendar but on the Hebrew lunar calendar. So the seven-year cycle of the Shemitah has to be based not on the Western year, but on the biblical Hebrew year. So no matter what date it is on the Western calendar, the Shemitah will always end on the twenty-ninth day of Elul on the Hebrew calendar, which, in the year 2008 fell on September 29, the day of the crash. But in other years, the same day in the biblical calendar would fall on a different date in the Western calendar."

"And...?"

"So what happens if we go back seven years from the greatest stock market crash in history, back to the other greatest stock market crash in history, the crash of 2001, the one directly triggered by 9/11. On what day did it fall *on the biblical Hebrew calendar?*"

"Tell me..."

"*On the twenty-ninth day of Elul.* It all happened on the twenty-ninth day of Elul...*the exact same day*...the one day of the biblical calendar ordained from ancient times to cause the wiping away of credit and debt."

"My God," I said, "both of them?"

"Both of them," he answered.

◆◆◆

Ana now appeared noticeably shaken, visibly pale. Nouriel paused from relaying the account to address her response. "What?" he asked.

"It's astounding," she replied. "The two greatest stock market crashes America had ever known, *both* taking place on the exact same biblical day, separated by the exact period of time ordained in the Bible, seven years to the day, both occurring on the one biblical day appointed for the wiping out of credit and debt. Absolutely stunning!" She paused to collect her thoughts.

"And nobody saw it?" she asked.

"Apparently not."

"You were right, Nouriel."

"What do you mean?"

"When you first came into my office and started telling me about this ancient mystery that was supposed to explain everything from 9/11 to Wall Street…to the global economy…to my bank account…I really thought you were crazy."

"I know."

"No, I mean *actually* crazy…*clinically* crazy."

"How could you not?"

"It was just way too out there. You'd hear something like this in the movies…or in novels about the supernatural, but not in real life. But I never…I never could have imagined…this."

"How *could* you have?"

"Accept my apology, Nouriel."

"There's no need. If I were in your place, I would have thought the same thing."

"It's just so mind-boggling."

"I know."

"September 17…"

"What about it?"

"It came up before," she said, "didn't it?"

"It did."

"Why did it come up before?"

"The Isaiah 9:10 Effect."

"That was it…the interest rates…September 17 was the day the Federal Reserve slashed the nation's interest rates."

"That's correct. It was the beginning of the extreme post-9/11 suppressing of interest rates…The first concrete act of defiance in the face of 9/11…and that which would lead to the economic collapse seven years later."

"So," she said, "that would mean that the Isaiah 9:10 Effect began on the day of the Shemitah."

"It would mean that," he replied, "wouldn't it?"

"And therefore," she said, "it would mean that it was on the day of the first stock market crash in 2001 that the seeds were sown for the second."

"And that would make sense," he said.

"Why would it make sense?"

"Because one Shemitah leads up to the next, and the first calamity leads to the second."

"Now *I* have a question for *you*, Nouriel."

"Ask it."

"The twenty-ninth of Elul comes around once every year. Correct?"

"Yes."

"But there's only *one* Elul 29 that can close the seven-year cycle. Only *one* could be the actual day of remission, the one that comes around only once every *seven years*. So on which Elul 29 did the stock market crash of 2008 take place?"

"I asked the prophet the same thing."

"And what did he say?"

"Yes."

"Yes?"

"It was the *one*. The crash of 2008 took place on that precise twenty-ninth of Elul that comes around once every seven years— on the one and only day that comes around once every seven years."

"Incredible!"

"And do you realize what that means?"

"What?" she asked.

"It means that the other crash, the one that happened seven years earlier, the one set off by 9/11, the other greatest stock market crash in history also took place on that exact twenty-ninth of Elul...that comes around only once every seven years."

"So then the two greatest Wall Street stock market crashes not only happened on the same day on the biblical calendar, and on the one day of the biblical year ordained to wipe away credit and debt, but each one fell seven years apart on the exact once-in-seven-years occurrence of that one Hebrew day. It's beyond amazing..."

"And yet real."

"And what else did the prophet tell you?"

◆◆◆

I asked him if the biblical Shemitah was still observed.

"Yes," he said, "in the form of ritual."

"Then was the ritual of the Shemitah taking place on the day of the crash?" I asked.

"It was," he answered. "As religious Jews were observing the conclusion of the Shemitah, closing the seventh year in ritual acts, symbolically wiping away their credits and debts, on the same day the force of a more mysterious Shemitah was operating, causing Wall Street to collapse and astronomical sums of credit and debt to be wiped away...not in symbol...but in reality."

"But the mystery of the Shemitah could not have been manifested if 9/11 had never happened...and just when it did...at that exact time. Without 9/11, the stock market would never have crashed on the twenty-ninth of Elul. So 9/11 had to be woven into the mystery of the Shemitah."

"It had to be," he answered, "and it was."

"And for the crash of 2008 to have happened seven years later, exactly seven biblical years later...to the day, all the key events from the fall of Lehman Brothers to the vote on Capitol Hill, to the actions of the Federal Reserve, to the entire global crisis—to every other event that affected the economic realm from politics to war to culture—every event had to also be a part of the same ancient mystery."

"They had to be part," he replied, "as they were."

"It's…" I couldn't finish the thought. I couldn't think of any word to describe what it was. Just at that point, the wind again picked up in intensity, sweeping rapidly over the fields and extending the pause in our conversation.

"And one more thing…one more thing to note," he said, turning to look directly into my eyes. "The Hebrew word *Shemitah* has one other meaning."

"Which is…"

"*The fall* or *the letting fall.*"

"As in a collapse?"

"As in a collapse. So you could translate *Shemitah* as *The Year of the Fall* or *The Year of Letting Fall.*"

"And that's the mystery of what happened, isn't it?"

"Yes…behind everything…the fall of the stock market…the fall of the housing market and credit market…the fall of commerce and business and trade—everything fell. Every bankruptcy, every foreclosure, every financial failure, every plunge of every major economic indicator, the global collapse itself—everything was a fall. And the entire global collapse began with the fall of Lehman Brothers."

"Which was not only a fall," I said, "it was a *letting fall.* The Federal Reserve decided to *let it fall.*"

"Yes."

"So the entire global collapse began with the American government performing an act of Shemitah."

"And it goes deeper still."

"How?"

"No human hands could have orchestrated the countless actions, reactions, and transactions required to cause Wall Street and the global economy to collapse and for everything to happen just as it did, at the exact times ordained in the ancient mystery."

"Then by the hand of…"

"…God," said the prophet. "It was His Shemitah. It was His *letting fall.*"

"His letting fall of…"

"The American economic world order. With the collapse of the global economy, new challenges to American power and leadership would be unleashed—a foreshadowing of the ultimate end of the American-led global order."

"And all triggered by 9/11," I said.

"And all a prophetic message," he replied, "just as it was in the days of the prophet Jeremiah as he gazed out at a land devastated, devoid of its fruits and harvests, as he fathomed the sign of the Shemitah, the sign given to the nation that has forgotten its foundations, placed its trust in its powers and prosperity, and ruled God out of its life."

"And now it appears again."

"As a sign to another nation that has likewise ruled God out of its life, a sign to give warning to that nation that apart from His presence, its blessings must turn into curses and its prosperity must become its judgment."

◆◆◆

We stopped speaking and just stood there…watching the wind sweep over the fields. It had to have been a good two minutes before the silence was broken…by the prophet…with a question. "Are you ready, Nouriel?"

"Ready?"

"For the next mystery?"

"I don't know. I'm still trying to absorb this one. It's a lot to take in."

"You have the seal?"

"Yes." So I returned it to him, and he, in turn, then handed me another.

"Are you sure you meant to give me this one?" I asked.

"Why?"

"It's the scroll."

"It is."

"You've already given it to me...two times before."

"And now a third."

"It's the Prophecy...Isaiah 9:10," I said. "So what am I supposed to see in it that I haven't already seen before?"

"Nothing," he said.

"What do you mean?"

"It's not in the seal; it's in the giving."

"I don't understand."

"How many times have I given it to you now?"

"Three times."

"So there comes a third."

"A third what?"

"A third witness."

Chapter 18

The Third Witness

א ח

THE THIRD WITNESS...THAT'S all he told me."

"So there was no other clue?" she asked.

"No."

"And that was the end of the encounter?"

"Yes. I headed back through the stalks of wheat to my car. The prophet remained...in the midst of the fields. Halfway there I turned back. He was still standing there in the distance...as when I first saw him.

"'Do you need a ride?' I shouted back.

"'To where?' he replied.

"'I don't know...maybe to the place of our next meeting.'

"'But then we wouldn't be able to meet there,' he replied.

"I reached the car and turned back again. He was still there. I began driving away. I looked back one more time...it had only been a few seconds into the drive...and he was gone."

"So you really didn't have much to go on this time."

"No, the slightest of clues and a seal I had already been given twice before. And I wasn't thinking about either, at first. I was still caught up in the mystery that had just been shown, trying to digest it all. It was about an hour into the drive before I began pondering the next one and the meaning of the seal.

"But I don't understand," she said. "How could you find anything more? It was already revealed to you twice. What else could it mean? And how were you supposed to figure it out?"

"That was the hard part. The seal was of the Ninth Harbinger, the scroll representing the Prophecy...the vow...as proclaimed from

Capitol Hill. The second time it was given, it still had to do with the vow, but now the repercussions of that vow, the Isaiah 9:10 Effect."

"So what would it mean given a third time?" she asked.

"Apart from the seal itself, I only had one clue."

"The third witness."

"Yes…but that's all I needed."

"How?"

"The first two witnesses had already been revealed."

"And that was enough for you to know where to go?"

"The seal was linked to a place. Where did each witness recite the vow?"

"In the capital."

"Exactly…and just when it hit me, I passed a sign."

"For Washington?"

"Yes."

"And you took the sign…as a *sign*?"

"How could I not take the sign as a sign?"

"Now you're sounding like the prophet."

"My journey changed. I took the exit and headed to Washington, and, specifically, to Capitol Hill. It was a couple of hours drive. When I arrived, it was late afternoon, early evening. I made my way to the Capitol Building, to the same steps on which the prophet revealed the Ninth Harbinger."

"And what happened?"

"What happened? What happened is he was there! He was already there!"

"But when you drove away, he was still in the field."

"Yes, and there was no vehicle in sight, apart from my car, yet he was there before me…waiting."

"Did you ever ask him how he did it?" she asked.

"No. It was enough for me to try to figure out the mysteries. To try to figure out the prophet on top of that would have been too much. So he was standing there on the terrace in the middle of the steps overlooking the mall. The sun had either just set or was just about to. The wind was as strong as it had been earlier that day. I made my way up the steps and joined him on the terrace."

‹—————————◆◆◆—————————›

"You did well to get here so fast," he said, as I approached.

"But you were still here before me."

"Do you remember when we first came here?"

"Of course," I replied. "It was when you told me of the Ninth Harbinger."

"The Ninth Harbinger—Isaiah 9:10 in the form of prophecy. Here the prophecy was proclaimed on the day after 9/11. Here the nation vowed the vow to emerge stronger than before. Seven years later the vow would be undone."

"With the collapse of the economy."

"Yes," he said. "And what event, more than any other, would bring about that collapse?"

"The fall of Lehman Brothers."

"And what decision was most critical in bringing about that fall?"

"The decision of the American government to let Lehman Brothers fall."

"And when was that decision announced?"

"I don't know."

"It happened on the first day of emergency meetings in New York City as the Treasury Secretary informed the leaders of Wall Street that the government had decided not to save the ailing firm. It would let Lehman Brothers fall. It was the most fateful of all decisions in triggering the collapse of the American and global economy. The decision was announced and sealed on the Friday before the collapse...September 12."

"September 12," I said. "That was the same day that..."

"The same day the prophecy was proclaimed on this hill. It was seven years from the proclamation of the vow to the announcement of the decision that would cause the collapse of its economy—to the day."

"So the economic collapse was triggered on the seventh anniversary of the proclaiming of the ancient vow."

"Just as in ancient times the same vow would ultimately lead to the collapse of ancient Israel."

"A very dangerous vow."

"Nouriel, do you remember the biblical requirement of witnesses?" he asked.

"For a truth to be established," I replied, "or a judgment pronounced, there must be two witnesses."

"Yes, but another number is also mentioned in Scripture:

> "By the mouth of two or *three* witnesses the matter shall be established.[1]

> "By the mouth of two or *three* witnesses every word shall be established.[2]

"So too in the matter of a nation's judgment. The first witness appears on the day after the calamity to proclaim the ancient prophecy from this hill. The second witness appears three years later to deliver a speech centered entirely around the same ancient prophecy. Each would connect 9/11 to Isaiah 9:10, America to ancient Israel. And each would vow: '*We will rebuild.*'

"Each unwittingly pronounces judgment on America. So two witnesses had spoken."

"But the Scriptures speak of a third...."

"So could there be a third witness...a third witness to confirm the connecting of the ancient prophecy to 9/11...but now also to the economic collapse...a third witness as a sign that the underlying course of judgment had not stopped but had progressed to a further stage? Could there be a third witness to speak from an even higher level and on an even greater scale?"

"Higher than the Senate majority leader?" I asked.

"Do you know where we are?"

"Capitol Hill."

"No, right here...on this terrace."

"No," I answered.

"This is the place where presidents are sworn into office.

"This is the place of the inauguration?"

"The inauguration—an event filled with hope and expectancy.

But in the case of a nation in departure from God and heading to judgment, hope can only come in repentance. Without a change of course, the end must remain the same, and all other hopes must fail."

"The third witness is..."

"The third witness is the president of the United States."

"How?" I asked.

"It's evening," he said. "February 24, 2009, the new president comes to this hill one month after his inauguration. He enters the chamber of the House of Representatives, makes his way down the aisle to the podium, and is greeted with thunderous applause. The nation's economy is still in a state of free fall, and a tangible sense of foreboding hangs over the future. Even before he utters his first word, the speech is being hailed as the most important address of his early presidency. It will be the first time he stands as president to address a joint session of Congress and the nation...and his moment to give America an answer to its greatest crisis since 9/11. The chamber quiets...he begins:

> "Madame Speaker, Mr. Vice President, Members of Congress, and the First Lady of the United States: I've come here tonight not only to address the distinguished men and women in this great chamber, but to speak frankly and directly to the men and women who sent us here. I know that for many Americans watching right now, the state of our economy is a concern that rises above all others.[3]

"After setting the stage and framing the magnitude of the crisis, the speech turns:

> "But while our economy may be weakened and our confidence shaken; though we are living through difficult and uncertain times, *tonight I want every American to know this—WE WILL REBUILD.*"[4]

"It's the vow," I said. "It's Isaiah 9:10!"

"And note the strangeness of it, Nouriel, the peculiarity of its appearance in such a context. *We will rebuild* was what was declared in the wake of 9/11. But in the midst of an economic crisis, it's hardly the most natural or the most fitting thing to say—except that it all fits into the deeper mystery…in which the two calamities are being joined together."

"And the president had no idea he was voicing the central declaration of Isaiah 9:10?"

"Did the first and second witnesses have any idea what they were saying?"

"No," I said, "but they knew they were quoting from Scripture."

"Still, they had no idea what it meant. In the case of the president, he had no idea he was quoting from anything. And he wasn't…he was seeking to inspire the nation. Nevertheless, out of his mouth came the central declaration of the ancient vow. That he proclaimed the same words without even having a quote to quote from is all the more striking."

"It just happened to happen," I replied, "just like everything else."

"It happened because it had to…one way or the other. The words had to manifest, one more link in the mystery, bearing witness that what started with 9/11 had not ended but was still in effect…and progressing."

It was now dark as we spoke on the terrace. The monuments of the Washington Mall were aglow with white, yellow, and orange light, as was the Capitol building itself.

The prophet continued, "The words '*we will rebuild*' had also manifested in the speech that launched the War on Terror, the speech given by the former president. But in that case the phrase was qualified and specific to the rebuilding of New York. But now the words would come forth with nothing to qualify or limit them— simply '*WE WILL REBUILD*.' Now, an American president would proclaim the central declaration of Israel's fateful vow as the central declaration of his entire address."

"But with nothing to qualify it," I asked, "how specifically could three words be linked to Isaiah 9:10?"

"Good question," he replied. "Imagine this experiment: Before the president's speech, you type in those three words into almost any major search engine on the Internet... *We will rebuild*...just those three words, and nothing else. What would happen? The search engine would take you to the ancient prophecy. That specific verse would, more than likely, appear in the first pages of results, if not on the very first page. That's how specifically the three words are joined to the ancient prophecy. But now it's the night of the speech. You repeat the experiment and type in the same three words, but now, instead of taking you to the ancient vow, it takes you to the words of the American president. As the night advances, you repeat the experiment. Each time you do it, you witness the president's vow progressively pushing the ancient vow farther and farther away from the top of the list, or, to put it another way, the vow of the American president now takes the place of the ancient vow."

"So the mystery was now playing out on the World Wide Web."

"Before a global audience; through television, radio, print, and the Internet; through the president of the United States in the hearing of the nation and much of the world. And just as it was with the first two witnesses, the vow would once more manifest as the climax and pinnacle of the speech in which it appeared."

"How," I asked, "without coming at the end of the speech?"

"Where it appeared in the speech was irrelevant. The president's address was picked up by news services around the world. Each had to choose a phrase to serve as a summation and headline. From the thousands of words contained in that speech, the words most often chosen to encapsulate and represent it were those of the ancient vow:

- "CBS News:
  Obama: '*We Will Rebuild.*'

- "CNN:
  Obama: '*We Will Rebuild.*'

- "MSNBC:
  Obama tonight: '*We Will Rebuild.*'

- "The *Guardian*:
  Obama: 'We will rebuild.'

- "National Public Radio:
  Obama Pledges: *'We Will Rebuild.'*

- "*Times Online:*
  Obama tells America: *'We will rebuild.'*

- "*Fox News*:
  Obama Says 'Country Will Rebuild.'

- "*Al Jazeera*:
  Obama pledges U.S. *'will rebuild.'*

- "*Drudge Report*:
  Obama Says 'USA Will Rebuild.'

- "Associated Press:
  Obama: *'We will rebuild.'*

- "*New York Times*:
  Obama Vows, *'We Will Rebuild.'*

- "Isaiah 9:10:
  'We will rebuild.'"

"From the *New York Times* to *Al Jazeera*," I said, "they all chose the central declaration of Isaiah 9:10...with no one having any idea."

"No more than the one who proclaimed it had any idea. The same principle that caused the Harbingers to manifest in the first place was now operating through the global media. And notice something else, Nouriel. The president didn't just say, *'We will rebuild.'* He prefaced it with this:

I want every American to know this: We will rebuild.[5]

"Does it sound familiar?"

"It's the prophetic address, that which comes before a prophetic utterance, to identify the person or people to whom it's being sent. So the word was now being sent to *every American*."

"Correct," he answered. "The ancient prophecy was addressed to the people of Israel:

"…and all the people will know it.[6]

"So now, the president of the United States is *readdressing* it. It is now given for *every American to know*. And as with the other witnesses, he too clearly identifies who the '*we*' is of *we will rebuild*. The president is reciting the vow on behalf of *every American*."

"And by doing that, the president is, in effect, identifying America as a nation estranged from God, in defiance of His will, and heading toward judgment."

"Yes," said the prophet, "just as did the first two witnesses. In order for a truth or a judgment to be established, there must be two or three witnesses, and the testimony of each must be consistent with that of the others. To that end, the president added a second line to his vow:

"We will rebuild, we will recover."[7]

"Why does it sound familiar?" I asked.

"On the day after 9/11, when the ancient vow was first proclaimed from Capitol Hill, the Senate majority leader sealed the vow and his address with these words:

"We will rebuild and we will recover."[8]

"So the president was repeating the words spoken on Capitol Hill," I said, "the day after 9/11. But he couldn't have done it purposely."

"No," said the prophet, "not purposely…but unknowingly, as with everything else. And notice…when the Senate majority leader proclaimed those two declarations, the words were not only being joined to the attack but clearly to Isaiah 9:10. And now the president utters the same words but now to speak of the economic collapse. So, the same declaration spoken over the first shaking is now spoken over the second. The two events are again joined together, and it's all joined together by Isaiah 9:10."

"And they both made their proclamations in the same place."

"Yes," he said, "the witnesses are joined together not only by their testimony but also by the place in which they give their testimony. Each of the three witnesses proclaims the vow in the capital city. The first and third witness proclaim the vow not only in the same city but also on the exact same hill."

"In the exact same building."

"And a building divided in two...into two wings...two chambers...the Senate and the House, the nation's two highest legislative assemblies...each of which must confirm a law or proclamation in order for it to be passed...as with two witnesses. And so the ancient vow is proclaimed, first from the floor of the Senate on the day after 9/11, and then from the floor of the House of Representatives...first from the northern wing and then from the southern, once in each wing...once in each chamber...two witnesses."

"And did the president say anything else that linked up with Isaiah 9:10?"

"Yes, with Isaiah 9:10 and with the commentaries. When the leaders of ancient Israel declared, '*The bricks have fallen, but we will rebuild*,' what were they saying?"

"Tell me."

"They were saying that fallen bricks would not decide their future, the crisis would not determine their nation's destiny—*they themselves* would. From the commentaries:

> "The arrogant response demonstrates how stubborn and overconfident the people of Israel were. *They thought they could determine their own destiny*.[9]

"So after declaring, '*We will rebuild*,' the president gave voice to another declaration:

> "The weight of this crisis will not *determine the destiny of this nation*.[10]

"It's *the bricks have fallen, but we will rebuild*, translated into modern political terminology."

"And what did he say *would* determine the nation's destiny?" I asked.

"America would be its own answer:

> "The answers to our problems don't lie beyond our reach. They exist in our laboratories and universities; in our fields and our factories; in the imagination of our entrepreneurs and the pride of the hardest-working people on Earth.[11]

"In other words, '*We will emerge from this crisis by relying on the greatness of our powers and resources...*'"

"*We will rebuild...with quarried stones*," I said, "*and cedar trees*."

"Exactly," he replied. "*We will determine our own destiny*. And yet the ancient vow boasted of more than that...more than rebuilding and more than recovering."

"It was about coming out of the crisis stronger than before."

"Exactly. And so the president would add one more declaration to his vow. Listen to the words:

> "We will rebuild, we will recover, *and the United States of America will emerge stronger than before*.[12]

"A perfect summation of the ancient prophecy. Now look what happens if you take the words of the president and hold them up against the words of a commentary on Isaiah 9:10:

- "From the commentary: 'They boasted that they would rebuild their devastated country.'[13]

- "From the president: '*We will rebuild, we will recover.*'[14]

- "The commentary: '...and make it stronger and more glorious than ever before.'[15]

- "The president: 'And the United States of America *will emerge stronger than before.*'"[16]

"It's scary," I said, "how closely it matches."

"Much scarier," said the prophet, "is what it all led to...in the ancient case."

"And in the modern case?" I asked.

"The answer to the nation's problems," he said, "lies *not* in its powers but in a Power much higher than these. And until—and unless—that answer and hope are found, every other answer and hope must fail in the end, and the prophecy must continue in effect, along with the progression of judgment."

"The progression of judgment...So things only get worse?"

"In the realm of appearance, not always. What followed 9/11 appeared to be an era of economic resurgence and expansion. But in reality it was a house of cards. A very different dynamic was at work beneath the surface...and progressing...until the cards collapsed."

"The Isaiah 9:10 Effect."

"The progression of judgment advances in times of calamity and crisis, but equally in times of apparent recovery, apparent normalcy, and even apparent resurgence, booming economies, and prosperity. None of it hinders or ends the progression. Whether above the surface or beneath it, the progression continues."

"Then what ends the progression?" I asked.

"Either judgment...or the answer."

"And it's heading to which?"

"To which end do you think, Nouriel?"

"It's heading away from God."

"The progression of judgment is only a reaction to the progression of a nation's apostasy, its progressive severing of its connection to

God and to the biblical foundation on which it was established. If the first progression doesn't end, then neither can the second."

————— ♦♦♦ —————

"So the answer is..."

"The seal," he replied.

"The answer is the seal?"

"May I have the seal?" he asked. So I gave it to him as he placed another in my right hand.

"This," he said, "is what I gave you at the beginning, the seal of the First Harbinger. We now leave the mysteries of the second shaking and move to the answer. And as this was the seal that opened up the first mysteries of the Harbingers, so too it will open up the last...and the answer."

"And this one is like all the other revelations...or not?"

"This one," he said, "is *unlike* all the other revelations...and yet all of them are joined to it."

"And where does one go to find its meaning?" I asked.

"Its meaning lies hidden...in the foundation."

"The foundation of what?"

"America."

"Where?"

"In the mystery ground."

Chapter 19

The Mystery Ground

א ה

"THE SEAL OF the First Harbinger," said Ana, "was of...what again?"

"The Breach," he replied. "The opening in the wall...the removal of the hedge of protection."

"But there had to be something else about it...something you didn't notice at the beginning."

"Exactly."

"And did you find it?"

"Yes, after examining it carefully, yes, it actually took a magnifying glass to make out the details."

"And what was it?"

"A very, very minute image at the bottom right-hand corner of the wall, a rectangle...a vertical rectangle...with a series of points running along the top as if some sort of crown."

"And what did you make of it?" she asked.

"At first, nothing more than that, a crown on a box."

"And what would a crown on a box signify?"

"I had no idea," he said. "So I went searching through countless books, collections, and compilations on symbols and imagery. But nothing appeared to match, nothing that made any sense. And then I found it, by accident...not by accident but by what appeared to be an accident at the time. I've long lost my faith in accidents."

"So what happened?"

"I was home, watching a documentary on ancient mysteries on television. And then it appeared on the screen."

"The crown on the box?"

"Yes."

"And what was it?"

"The Temple of Jerusalem. If you approached it from the front, that's what it would look like...a vertical rectangle with a line of golden spikes on top."

"And what did you make of it?"

"There was the Temple, and there was the breach. So putting it together...a breach...in the Temple."

"A breach in the Temple of Jerusalem?"

"It couldn't have been the Temple of Jerusalem," he replied, "not literally. The mystery concerned America. So I took the Temple to be the representation of a holy place...a church...a synagogue...a shrine...some holy place."

"A breach in a holy place?"

"Yes. So I began searching for anything having to do with a breach in a house of worship...and of significance for America."

"And?"

"And after much searching...nothing. So I returned to Battery Park."

"Why?" she asked.

"Because it was there that the prophet first revealed the meaning of that first seal."

"And...?"

"And nothing. Time passed. I was growing discouraged. And then something happened...a clue came to me...in a way nothing had ever come to me before."

"What do you mean?"

"A dream. It came to me in a dream."

"Interesting."

"It was a dream of the Temple of Jerusalem. The day was sunny. The Temple courts were filled with people, multitudes...thousands and thousands of people dressed in robes, all gathered for some sort of event...some celebration. There was a procession. In the procession was a golden object. It had to be the Ark of the Covenant.

"How did you know it was the Ark of the Covenant?" she asked.

"I've seen the movies," he replied. "There were musicians playing trumpets and harps and sounding cymbals as the people sang in worship. A cloud filled the Temple...not a regular cloud...but some kind of supernatural cloud of radiance. There was a man standing on some sort of platform near the Temple. He turned around to face the multitudes and began addressing them. It was the king—King Solomon."

"And how did you know it was King Solomon?"

"He was wearing a crown and what seemed to be a royal robe of gold. And I just knew, the way you just know things in a dream...intuitively."

"So King Solomon was speaking to the crowd...and saying what?"

"I couldn't tell or understand. But after he finished speaking, he turned back toward the Temple, knelt down, covered his head with the golden robe, and lifted his hands to the sky. He was praying. He was leading the people in prayer. And as they prayed, I was walking through their midst...through crowds...toward the platform where the king was kneeling. I approached him. He was now just a few feet away from me. But I could only see him from the back since he was turned in the opposite direction. He stood up, still facing the Temple and with the golden robe still covering his head. And then he turned around, I saw his face...and it wasn't him."

"What do you mean *it wasn't him*?" she asked.

"It wasn't King Solomon anymore," he answered.

"Then who was it?"

"It was Washington."

"Washington...as in the president?"

"Washington," said Nouriel, "as in George. He let the robe fall to his side. And he stood there on the platform looking just as you'd picture him—a white powdered wig, a dark brown waistcoat and breeches, white silk stockings, and dark shoes with silver buckles. He lifted up both hands to the heavens just as Solomon had done, closed his eyes, and began to pray. When he finished praying, he opened his eyes and lowered his right hand as if reaching for something in front of him, but there was nothing there. Then a sheet of paper descended from the sky and landed in his left hand, which was still raised upward. Just at that moment he lowered his glance and appeared to be looking directly into my eyes. He then descended the steps of the platform and walked over to the Temple, still holding the paper in his hand. When he reached the corner of the building, he bent down and slipped the paper into one of the cracks in between two massive stones, where it disappeared. As it disappeared, he faded away. I looked around toward the multitude, but they too were gone."

"And then what?"

"Then I was alone...standing in the Temple courts. The sky began to darken. The winds began blowing stronger and stronger. It seemed that time itself was accelerating faster and faster until all around me was a whirlwind of action, events, and sound...an intense blur of sight and sound...as the sky continued to darken and darken until it was almost as dark as night. Whatever was happening, it didn't seem to be a good thing. And then it was over, as if a violent storm had just passed through. The darkness began to break and everything was growing brighter. But when I turned back to see the Temple, it was gone. It was in ruins...its massive stones scattered on the mount. Everything was destroyed. It was then that I noticed a man...turned away from me...a man in a golden robe."

"The golden robe of King Solomon?"

"Yes. He was standing in the same place where Washington stood before he disappeared...at the corner of the Temple, except that now there was no corner and no Temple...only ruins, but it was the same place. At the man's feet was a sheet of paper, the paper that had been hidden inside the stones. But the destruction had caused it to be revealed. He bent down to pick it up. I felt I had to approach him, and as I did, he turned around—and it was him!"

"Solomon?"

"No."

"Washington?"

"No."

"Then who?"

"It was the prophet."

"The prophet..."

"The golden robe dropped to his side, revealing his long dark coat. He looked into my eyes, then handed me the paper. I took it into my hands and looked down to see what it said."

"And what did it say?" she asked.

"I don't know."

"Why not?"

"Because I woke up!"

"Bad timing," she replied.

"I don't know," he said. "I think it was meant to happen just as it did."

"The mystery you were seeking...the prophet told you it was hidden in the foundation. So the paper in the dream, it was hidden in the wall of a building."

"That struck me as well," he replied.

"So you believed the dream was significant...a sign?"

"I did."

"So what did you make of it?"

"It all centered on the Temple. The Temple was on the seal. The seal was about a breach, the removal of protection...destruction. The dream involved the destruction of the Temple."

"But what about George Washington?" she asked. "What would be the meaning of his appearance?"

"Solomon was the king of Israel. Washington was the first president of the United States. There was something in the linking of ancient Israel and America, as with all the other mysteries."

"And the paper?"

"As you said—the mystery hidden in the foundation, a message concerning America, waiting to be uncovered."

"So where did it all lead you?"

"I had no idea where it was all leading me. And then it hit me...Washington! Washington hid the mystery. So the mystery was hidden in Washington...the city...the nation's foundation. And the Temple was in Jerusalem, which was the capital. The mystery again pointed to the capital city. So I returned to Washington DC."

"But looking for what this time?"

"For any connection to the Temple or King Solomon. But the search came up with nothing, so I expanded it to include any house of worship of significance. But again, nothing. So I expanded it again to include now any place with a specific connection to George Washington—the Washington Monument, the statue in the middle of the Capitol Rotunda."

"And…?"

"Again, nothing. So finally I just went searching everywhere—the Smithsonian, the Jefferson Memorial, the Supreme Court… everywhere."

"And…?"

"Yet again… nothing."

"So how long were you there in Washington?"

"Several weeks. And then I gave up. I returned home discouraged. The dream appeared to be filled with clues, but there was nothing to connect any of them to anything meaning anything. So I returned again to the only place with a definite connection to the seal."

"Battery Park?"

"Yes. And that's where I was, standing… by the water's edge, watching a seagull in the sky when I heard the voice again from behind me."

"The prophet?"

"The prophet."

◆◆◆

"You haven't given up," he said, "have you, Nouriel?"

"Why does it look like I have?" I asked.

"I didn't say it did," he replied.

"You know, there's a fine line," I said, "between giving up and having absolutely nothing to go on."

"So you think you have absolutely nothing to go on?"

"It's not that I *think* I have absolutely nothing to go on… but what I do have to go on doesn't go anywhere."

"Then tell me what you do have"

"The Temple of Jerusalem… the capital city… a breach… a holy place… destruction… Washington DC…"

"And nothing else?"

"That's about it."

"Why don't we go for a little walk?" So we began walking, first through Battery Park and then out into the streets of Lower Manhattan.

"The Temple of Jerusalem was the house of God's glory," said the prophet. "But in 586 B.C., after centuries of apostasy and with no hope of return, the Lord finally allowed His house to be touched by judgment and destroyed."

"The Temple and the breach, the destruction of the Temple, that much I had right."

"The Temple was the focal point of the nation's life. So the focal point of the nation's judgment…"

"…would be the Temple's destruction."

"Exactly."

"So as went the Temple, so went the nation."

"For good or bad. When the Temple's construction was completed by King Solomon, the kingdom itself was complete."

"Solomon…"

"And when he dedicated it to God, it was the nation as well that was dedicated."

"I saw it!" I said, my voice rising in pitch.

"What do you mean?" he asked.

"That's what it was in the dream—the dedication of the Temple. I had a dream, and it began with Solomon leading a gathering of multitudes at the Temple."

"Interesting," said the prophet.

"Tell me, what exactly did Solomon do on the day he dedicated the Temple?"

"He gathered the nation and its leaders to Jerusalem. He addressed the gathering, reminding them of how faithful God had been to the nation. Then he offered up prayers, prayers for the future generations. Solomon was looking into the nation's future, foreseeing its coming departure from God and its consequences."

"The consequences being…"

"The removal of God's favor from the land," said the prophet, "the withdrawal of His blessings...the nation's hedge of protection...national calamity."

"And it all happened?" I asked.

"Yes. The prayers of King Solomon were prophetic. But he wasn't only foretelling what would happen to those future generations; he was also praying on their behalf, in light of what would happen, for God's mercy and for restoration."

"So he was praying in view of calamities—which hadn't even happened?"

"That was the point. It wasn't only the Temple that was being dedicated on that day, but the nation's future, its generations yet to be born. The Temple Mount was the nation's ground of dedication."

"I saw it all in my dream.... And after the dedication, the sky turned dark and something like a storm was coming. And at the end of the storm, the Temple was destroyed. There was nothing left but ruins."

"Which is exactly what happened. A spiritual darkness engulfed the land, and the nation departed from God. And then, after years and years of mercy, the judgment fell. And that judgment was only complete when it touched the Temple Mount, the same place where the nation's future had been consecrated to God, the same place its apostasy had been foretold. The Lord had allowed the judgment to strike the nation's most sacred ground, the ground of its consecration. This, Nouriel, is a critical principle. Take note of it. When judgment comes to such a nation once committed to God and once consecrated to His purposes, but now departed from His ways, the judgment will return to its ground of consecration, or to put it more concisely:

> "The nation's ground of consecration will become the ground of its judgment."

"Why?" I asked

"The Temple Mount represented the nation's covenant with God. So its destruction was the ultimate sign that the covenant was broken. Yet even in that there was mercy. It was a sign that

God was calling the nation back, to remember the ground of its dedication and consecration to Him...the foundation on which all of its blessings rested."

"So it was both a sign of judgment," I said, "and a prophetic message calling the nation back...to return to the foundation."

"Correct."

I took out the seal to look at it once more. "But what does it all have to do with America?" I asked.

"On the day after 9/11," he said, "the Senate majority leader recited the words of the ancient prophecy at the *end* of his speech. But at the *beginning* of that speech, he cited a number. He said:

> "It is with pain, sorrow, anger, and resolve that I stand before this Senate—a symbol for 212 years of the strength of our Democracy.[1]

"Notice the number, Nouriel."

"Two hundred twelve."

"It was given to connect 9/11 to the founding of the American government, the establishment of the American nation-state. Do the math."

"Two thousand one, minus 212 years, comes to 1789."

"Correct. 1789."

"But I thought America was founded in 1776."

"The year 1776 was the year America declared its independence. It would be several years before that independence became a reality, and several more years before there was a Constitution upon which the nation would be established. America, as we know it—with a president, a Senate, and a House of Representatives—only came into existence in 1789. More specifically, it came into existence on April 30, 1789, the day when, for the first time, all these were in place—America's first day as a fully constituted nation."

"What happened on April 30?"

"It was the day that the nation's government was completed as set forth in the Constitution, the day America's first president was inaugurated."

"George Washington!"

"Yes."

"He was part of it too," I said. "He was there in the dream...at the dedication of the Temple. First it was King Solomon, and then it was Washington."

"Why do you think that was, Nouriel?"

"Why was Washington in my dream?"

"Yes."

"Tell me."

"It wasn't *my* dream."

"I don't know," I said. "A sign that it had something to do with America."

"What was he doing in your dream?"

"Leading the people in prayer, like Solomon. And then he stretched out his hand as if reaching for something."

"Like this?" The prophet stretched forth his right hand with his palm turned down.

"Yes, exactly like that. How did you..."

"But he wasn't so much reaching for something; his palm was turned down."

"Then what was he doing?" I asked.

"He was placing his hand on a Bible," said the prophet, "to swear. He was taking the oath of the presidency. It was the inauguration, April 30, 1789, the beginning of America as a constituted nation—the foundation, 212 years before 9/11."

"The inauguration of George Washington on the Temple Mount?"

"In your dream the two events were joined together—Israel's dedication and America's inauguration, the one superimposed on the other."

"Why?"

"It was *your* dream...you tell me."

"Because somehow the two days are connected?"

"But how?" asked the prophet. "What would they have in common?"

"The dedication of the Temple was also an inauguration," I said, "and the inauguration of the American government would also be a type of dedication. Each was an opening day and a day of completion. Each represented the completion of a structure...the structure of a nation. And each involved the nation gathering together."

"Gathering together where?"

"In the nation's capital?"

"And who presided over each gathering?"

"The nation's leader...the king...the president."

"And in your dream, did King Solomon speak?"

"Yes."

"What did he say?"

"I don't know."

"King Solomon began his address by acknowledging God's hand and faithfulness in the nation's history. So, on America's inauguration day, the nation's first president would do likewise. In the first ever presidential address, this is what he said:

> "No people can be bound to acknowledge and adore the Invisible Hand which conducts the affairs of men more than those of the United States. Every step by which they have advanced to the character of an independent nation seems to have been distinguished by some token of providential agency.[2]

"As he addressed the people in the days of the dedication, King Solomon offered up prayers and supplications to the Almighty, interceding for the Lord's blessing on the nation's future. Now listen to the words of Washington's first presidential address:

> "It would be peculiarly improper to omit in this first official act my fervent supplications to that Almighty Being who rules over the universe, who presides in the councils of nations, and whose providential aids can supply every human defect, that His benediction may consecrate to the liberties and happiness of the people of the United States a Government instituted by themselves for these essential purposes.[3]

"In my dream, Solomon was praying, then Washington took his place but continued praying. The two leaders...the two events were superimposed. So that's why."

"And it wasn't just Solomon who was praying for the nation's future," he said, "but all the leaders and multitudes who were gathered on the Temple Mount, everyone. So too it was on America's inauguration. It was designated as a day of prayer and dedication. This was the proclamation that went forth:

> "On the morning of the day on which our illustrious President will be invested with his office, the bells will ring at nine o'clock, when the people may go up to the house of God and in a solemn manner commit the new government, with its important train of consequences, to the holy protection and blessing of the Most High. An early hour is prudently fixed for this peculiar act of devotion and is designed wholly for prayer.[4]

"So, on the morning of April 30, 1789, the sounds of bells filled the nation's capital for thirty minutes, calling the people to *go up to the house of God, to commit the new government to the holy protection and blessing of the Most High.* As for the nation's first president and government, it would be later that same day that they would gather for prayer to commit the future into God's hands, at a place especially chosen for that purpose. So after the new president finished delivering the first presidential address, he would lead the Senate and the House of Representatives on foot in a procession through the streets of the capital from Federal Hall, the site of the inauguration, to the place appointed for their prayers."

"And what was the place appointed?" I asked.

"A little stone church."

"So the first official act of the newly formed government took place inside the walls of a church."

"That's correct," he replied. "The nation's first president, Senate, and House of Representatives were all there inside that little stone sanctuary. The gathering would be recorded in the Annals of

Congress as part of the first-ever joint session of Congress with an acting president. The inauguration of the United States, as we know it, began with a sacred gathering before God."

"So the first collective act of the newly formed American government was to gather for prayer."

"To gather for prayer, undoubtedly to give thanks, and specifically to commit the future into *the holy protection and blessing of the Most High*."

Just then we came to a stop at a street corner. "It's time," he said. "It's time to uncover the last piece of the mystery. To do that, we must identify the ground."

"The ground?"

"The ground on which America was committed in prayer to God that first day."

"But there's something I'm not getting," I said. "All this happened in the capital city. Correct?"

"That's correct," he replied.

"Then what are we doing *here*?" I asked. "We were there in Washington DC, on Capitol Hill, even on the terrace where the presidents are inaugurated. Why didn't you show me this then when we were there? And even after that, when I returned to Washington, I was there for weeks, and you never showed up. But you show up *now*...I don't understand."

"You were right, Nouriel," he said. "The mystery *is* linked to the capital. You just came up with the wrong one."

"What do you mean—the wrong one?"

"When the nation began, its capital city wasn't Washington DC. On April 30, 1789, the city of Washington didn't exist."

"Then what was America's original capital city?" I asked.

"You're standing in it," he replied.

"New York? New York City?"

"The first capital of the United States was New York City. That's where it all took place."

"Washington was sworn in as president in New York City?"

"Yes," he replied. "Now I have someone to show you."

"Someone?"

He took me around the corner and down the street. There was a statue in the distance. "Do you recognize him?" he asked.

"Washington?"

"Correct."

It was the dark bronze statue of George Washington that stands on Wall Street facing the New York Stock Exchange. We drew nearer, coming to a stop just short of the platform on which it rested. From there we gazed up at the dark stoic figure.

"My dream!" I said. "This is exactly how he looked in my dream. He wasn't as big, but I was looking up at him the same way...from the same angle. And his right hand was extended just like that."

"And turned downward just like that," he said, "to rest on the Bible."

"I went all around Washington DC looking for anything connected to him—a statue, a monument, a clue—and this one didn't even occur to me."

"And why should it have?" he replied. "You're a New Yorker. Just because something's right in front of your eyes doesn't mean you have to see it. Washington never set foot in Washington DC, but he set foot here. This is where it all began. This is where the United States of America, as we know it, came into existence."

"In New York City."

"In New York City...and here."

"Here?"

"Here," he replied, "as in *right* here. There's an inscription on the pedestal. Read it, Nouriel. Read it out loud."

So I did:

> On this site in Federal Hall, April 30, 1789 George Washington took the Oath as the First President of the United States of America.[5]

"*On this site*...I've seen this statue so many times and never stopped to think about why it was here."

"Here is where it all happened: April 30, 1789, the streets and rooftops are overflowing with people. Washington places his hand on the Bible and swears the oath. The crowd breaks out in cheers, cannons boom, and bells ring out across the city. Then he withdraws into Federal Hall where he delivers the first presidential address before Congress. After that, he leads the nation's first government on foot in a procession to the little stone sanctuary to commit the nation's future in prayer to God."

"Where?" I asked.

"That's the key," he replied.

"The key to the mystery?" I asked.

"Yes."

"It would be the ground on which the nation was committed to God, the nation's ground of consecration."

"Correct."

"So it would have to be somewhere in New York City."

"A safe assumption."

"And if we're standing on the site where the inauguration took place...and they went by foot to the appointed place...then it couldn't be far from here."

"No it couldn't be," he replied.

And that's where I stopped, instead of following it through to its logical conclusion.

♦♦♦

"Why?" asked Ana. "Why would you stop just then?"

"Because I wasn't sure I was ready to see it or to know what the answer was."

"But you were searching for it all along," she said.

"Yes," he replied, "but it was never within my grasp before that moment. Did you ever get so close to something you were searching for, and when you know you're just about to find it...when it's in your reach, you're not sure you're ready to find it?"

"I think I understand," she said.

"That's what it was...I knew it was something very big, very central, and very important...but I wasn't sure I was ready to find it."

"So what happened?" she asked.

"The prophet didn't give me a choice."

———— ◆◆◆ ————

"Come, Nouriel," he said. "It's time to see the place where it all happened…America's ground of consecration. Let's follow in their steps as the president led them through the streets of the city on foot to the appointed place. Let's go."

So we walked down Wall Street and then onto another. I could picture it all as it happened two centuries earlier: Washington, the first senators, the first representatives, the first cabinet, America's first government, all heading to the sacred gathering. But it was now just me and the prophet, retracing the journey. Not that there weren't others on those same streets. There were, of course, but not with same purpose. I was silent the entire time, as was he. And then he stopped and turned to me. "There it is, Nouriel," he said, pointing to a building across the street. "There it is. The place where America was dedicated to God."

The place was surrounded by a dark wrought-iron fence.

"Is that the same little stone church?"

"Yes," he answered.

The building was distinctive looking and yet, at the same time, in view of what it represented, inconspicuous. In the front was a columned, classical-looking façade. In the back was a steeple, tall, narrow, and more what you'd expect to find in an old church building.

"You might not even notice it," I said.

"What you're looking at, Nouriel, is St. Paul's Chapel. It stands now much as it did on April 30, 1789, when America's first government entered through its doors. It was here that the nation's first president, Senate, and House of Representatives bowed together in prayer to consecrate the new nation's future into the hands of God. This is the place where the new nation was committed to the Almighty; this is America's ground of consecration."

Then he was silent, letting me take it in. But I knew that wasn't the end of it. I knew there was something to be revealed, something he was holding back from telling me. "Originally, it faced the other way," he said. "Its front was in the back. Its main entrance was on the other side. Let's continue our walk."

So we crossed the street and walked along the sidewalk that lined the church's iron fence to our right. Within the iron fence was an old courtyard. As we walked, I found myself unable to stop peering through the bars at the trees, the grass, and the ancient-looking gravestones inside, looking for something significant to the mystery. I was still gazing into the courtyard as we neared the rear corner of the property.

"In the early days," the prophet said, "this is what you'd walk through to enter the sanctuary."

He allowed me just a few moments before speaking again.

"Turn around, Nouriel," he said.

"Let me just…" I was so focused on what was inside the fence that I didn't notice what was surrounding it.

"You're missing it," he said in a more somber tone. "It's right here, and you're missing it. Turn around."

So I turned around.

"Look," he said.

When I saw it, I was stunned to the point of almost losing my balance.

"Do you know what you're looking at?"

"It's not…"

"It's not *what*?"

"It's not…"

"What is it that it's not?"

"Ground Zero."

"But it *is* Ground Zero."

"Ground Zero…the last piece of the mystery."

"America's consecration ground," he said.

"Ground Zero," I repeated, unable, at that moment, to say anything else.

"America," he said, "was committed to God at the corner of what would become Ground Zero. It was here, at Ground Zero, that they all gathered—George Washington, John Adams, America's Founding Fathers. They all came here to the corner of Ground Zero to pray on the day that America's foundation was laid...as the consecrating act of that foundation. It was here that they came to commit the nation's future to God's *holy protection*. And it was here where that holy protection would be withdrawn."

I removed the seal from my coat pocket to once more examine its image. It was then that its meaning hit me with a new and stark clarity. "The sacred ground...the nation's hedge of protection broken...and the ancient principle...*the ground of dedication becomes the ground of calamity...the judgment returns to the ground of consecration*."

"And literally so," said the prophet, "as the massive white cloud born of the destruction literally engulfed the little chapel and the debris and ashes of the falling towers covered its soil."

"So on this ground is hidden a national mystery. This is the mystery you spoke of, and in my dream...hidden in America's foundation."

The prophet pointed into the distance. "Had we been there on that day of inauguration, everything over there, everything beyond that point, would have been water. But between here and the water was a field...now known as *Ground Zero*...a field owned by a church. Ground Zero was originally church land."

"Owned by *what* church?" I asked.

"The same that operated out of St. Paul's Chapel."

"So then it was, in essence, one property...as one ground?"

"As one ground," he replied. "As one ground on the day America was consecrated there. Thus, it's not only that America's ground of consecration is *at* Ground Zero; America's ground of consecration *is* Ground Zero."

◆◆◆

"The mystery ground," said Ana, softly and with a distant look in her eyes as she pondered the implications of what she was hearing. "The mystery ground is Ground Zero."

"Ana, you haven't said anything up to now."

"Because I've been speechless," she replied. "It's so...I can't even say what it is.... I can't put it into words. I'm beyond speechless."

"That's how I felt when he told me all this."

"You never went there before," she asked, "to Ground Zero?"

"No. Not after my encounters with the prophet began."

"Why not?"

"I believe I was avoiding it."

"Why?"

"I think because it was too intense...too raw...too much the center of everything. I avoided it."

"So what happened after the prophet revealed the mystery of Ground Zero?"

"He led me around the corner and along the side of the dark metal fence that had once faced the North Tower. There was a gate leading to the courtyard behind the chapel. He ushered me in through the gate and led me through the courtyard, covered with grass and gravestones, over to an object that was on display."

◆◆◆

"Do you know what this is, Nouriel?" he asked.

"A tree trunk?" I answered.

"It's the Sycamore."

"*The Sycamore of Ground Zero?*"

"What's left of it. This is where they placed it, putting it on display for the public to see, having no idea of its ancient significance."

"*The sycamores have been cut down.*"

"The Sixth Harbinger."

"And on 9/11 where was it? Where was it struck down?"

He led me back toward the gate that bordered Ground Zero, then over to the right toward one of the courtyard's corners, until we stood under the branches of an evergreen.

"Here," he said. "This is where it stood and where it was struck down."

"It was struck down inside the courtyard of St. Paul's Chapel?"

"Yes."

"On the same ground where America was committed to God?"

"Yes, on the same ground."

"So the Harbinger was manifested on the nation's ground of consecration."

"Yes."

"And would that mean that this tree…"

"…yes, what you're looking at is the tree that was planted in its place."

"This is the Erez Tree?"

"Yes."

"But we will plant cedars in their place."

"It was right here," said the prophet, "over this fence that they lowered it into the ground where the Sycamore had stood up until being struck down on 9/11. And it was here where they gathered to hallow it."

"And to name it *the Tree of Hope.*"

"Yes."

"Not much of a Tree of Hope."

"No."

"And so the striking down of the Sycamore and the planting of the Erez Tree, the Sixth and Seventh Harbingers, were each manifested on America's ground of consecration?"

"The ancient principle—*the ground of consecration becomes the ground of judgment.*"

At that, he paused, allowing me again some time to take in everything I was seeing.

"There was something else in my dream," I said, "something that hasn't been explained."

"Which is what?" he asked.

"A sheet of paper that came down from the sky and into Washington's hand. On receiving it, he walked over to one of the corners, one of the corners of the Temple, and placed it in a crack in the wall where it disappeared. And then, after the destruction, the paper reappeared. And it was *you.*"

"It was *me?*"

It was *you* holding the paper. And then you handed it to me."

"And what did it say?"

"I don't know," I replied. "I woke up."

"Bad timing," said the prophet.

———◆◆◆———

"The prophet used those words?" she asked. "He actually said, '*Bad timing*'?"

"Yes."

"Those were the same words that *I* used, when you told me the same thing."

"Yes, but he said them *before* you did."

"So did he tell you the meaning of the paper?"

"He told me it was a message, and the fact that it descended from the sky signified that it was a message from God, a prophetic message."

"And what did it mean," she asked, "that it was placed inside the wall?"

"It meant that the message was hidden in the foundation, America's foundation, on the *day* of the nation's foundation..."

"April 30, 1789. And the one who hid it was..."

"Washington...as in my dream."

"There's a prophetic message hidden in America's foundation, and it was placed there by George Washington?" she asked.

"Yes," he replied.

"And the message was revealed at the end of your dream. So then the message is meant to be revealed?"

"Yes."

"When?" she asked.

"In the dream, it was revealed after a calamity that touched the nation's ground of consecration. The destruction revealed it."

"September 11 was the calamity that touched the nation's ground of consecration."

"Yes."

"So 9/11 somehow is linked to a prophetic message hidden in America's foundation?"

"September 11 struck the ground where America was consecrated to God. It pointed back to day of the consecration, April 30, 1789. But April 30, 1789, was also a day of prophecy, the day a prophetic message was given to the newly formed nation."

"What prophetic message?" she asked.

"It was the prophet, in my dream, who handed me the paper that Washington had hidden. So it would be the prophet who would reveal to me the contents of that message, but not before revealing something else that happened on 9/11."

◆◆◆

"America," said the prophet, "was dedicated as a nation on this ground to God. But it was in Federal Hall that America, as a nation, was founded. On April 30, 1789, the two places were joined together, and once more on September 11, 2001."

"How so?" I asked.

"When the towers fell, a shock wave was sent forth from Ground Zero to Federal Hall. The impact was so great that it opened up cracks in the foundation."

"Cracks in the foundation? In the foundation of the nation's foundation?"

"As if 9/11 was pointing everything back to that first day, to that first foundational day...to what happened at St. Paul's Chapel and what happened there in Federal Hall. And what was Federal Hall?"

"The place of Washington's inauguration and the nation's foundation."

"And where was that message hidden in your dream?"

"In the foundation."

"And so it was there, at Federal Hall, that the prophetic word was spoken."

"By Washington?" I asked.

"Yes, in the first words a president would ever speak to the nation, in the first-ever presidential address."

"Just as King Solomon, on the day of dedication, gave a prophetic message concerning his nation's future."

"So Washington also gave a prophetic message concerning America's future, waiting for a future generation and appointed for the day of calamity, waiting to be revealed—a message less than thirty words long, and yet one of the most important messages ever given to the nation."

"And the message..."

"The message is this:

"The propitious smiles of Heaven can never be expected on a nation that disregards the eternal rules of order and right which Heaven itself hath ordained.[6]

"*The propitious smiles of Heaven.* What do you think that would mean, Nouriel?"

"Heaven," I replied, "would be a way of referring to God."

"Yes. And *the propitious smiles of Heaven?*"

"...would mean God's blessing and favor."

"Correct. And *the eternal rules of order and right which Heaven itself has ordained?*"

"Would mean God's unchanging standards of morality...what's right and wrong."

"Good, Nouriel. Now put it together. What is it saying?"

"If America upholds God's eternal standards and follows His unchanging ways, then it will be blessed with His favor...His protection...His prosperity....But if America should depart from the ways of God, if it should disregard His eternal standards, then the smiles of heaven, the blessings of God, will be withdrawn—its prosperity, its protection, and its powers would be taken away. He's giving a warning to the nation: The day America turns away from God will be the day that begins the removing of its blessings."

"Correct," he said. "And his words would be prophetic on several counts. America would be blessed with God's favor as no other nation had ever been blessed. But the day would come when the nation would do exactly as it was warned never to do."

"It would *disregard the eternal rules of order and right that heaven itself has ordained.*"

"Yes," said the prophet. "It would declare those eternal rules to be an offense and would strike them down. And the words of the warning would come true. The smiles of heaven would begin to fade…the blessings of God would be withdrawn."

"September 11—the removal of America's protection, the economic collapse, the failing of American prosperity."

"And each blessing would be removed on a site connected to that first inaugural day, the day of the warning, Ground Zero at St. Paul's—the nation's ground of consecration—and the crash of the New York Stock Exchange at Federal Hall—the site of America's foundation—where the warning was given."

"That statue of Washington," I said, "standing right in front of the New York Stock Exchange, it's a memorial, a witness of the day the warning was given, right in front of the New York Stock Exchange, the symbol of America's prosperity…as it collapsed."

"A silent witness that the *smiles of Heaven* were being withdrawn."

We walked out the courtyard and stood by the gate.

"Look around, Nouriel," said the prophet as he pointed toward Ground Zero. "When the calamity struck, all of these buildings, all the buildings surrounding Ground Zero, were either destroyed or badly damaged, all the buildings except for one. There was only one building that escaped the calamity virtually untouched. It was called *the miracle of 9/11.*"

"And that building…"

"Was the stone sanctuary where America had been committed to God, St. Paul's Chapel. It was another silent witness pointing the nation back to its foundation."

"How did it happen," I asked, "that it was spared?"

"It was a single object," he said, "a tree."

"Not the…"

"The Sycamore…the Sycamore of Ground Zero."

"The Harbinger."

"The Sycamore was credited with having shielded the chapel

both from the force of the implosion and the flying wreckage of the falling towers."

"So the chapel was saved from destruction by the Harbinger?"

"Does that seem strange?" he asked.

"I don't know."

"The purpose of the Harbingers is not to condemn America to judgment but to save it, to give it warning, to awaken it, and to turn it back from destruction. The Sixth Harbinger saved the chapel. So too redemption comes not only apart from calamity…but also through it."

We resumed walking alongside the wrought-iron fence and around the courtyard.

"In the days after 9/11, a strange thing happened. People from all over the city and all over the nation were drawn here. First were the relief workers who used the chapel as a center for emergency operations. But then came the others, the grieving, the hurting, the curious, those seeking an answer. The chapel and the land on which it stood became the spiritual focal point of the calamity. Some wandered through the courtyard seeking consolation; others entered the sanctuary. This iron fence was covered over with pictures, messages, and objects of faith. And it wasn't that anyone fully knew exactly what it was that drew them there. It had nothing to do with anything taking place within its walls or with those now overseeing or officiating over its functions. It had to do with the place itself. There was something about it. And so they returned, unknowingly to pray on the same ground on which the nation's first leaders had also prayed on the day of the prophetic warning, which had now come to pass."

"It's as if…as if behind everything—behind Ground Zero, behind Federal Hall, behind the Chapel, behind the Harbingers—behind everything is the word *return!*"

"Not *as if*, Nouriel; it *is* the word behind everything. It's the word of the prophets. Behind every mystery and Harbinger a voice was calling, calling the nation back to God, and crying out, '*Return.*'"

Chapter 20

Things to Come

א ה

H E LED ME across the street to the heart of Ground Zero. It was surrounded by partitions and barriers, but from various positions one could see inside.

"All this, Nouriel," said the prophet, "was covered in ruins and fallen bricks."

"The bricks have fallen..."

"And do you see that?"

"The building?" I asked.

"Yes."

"Is that the Tower?"

"The beginning of the Tower," he replied. *"'But we will rebuild with Gazit Stone.'"*

"And where was the Gazit Stone?"

"Over there," he said. "That's where they lowered it. That's where they gathered together, and that where's they proclaimed their vows."

"And what happens next?" I asked. "If the first stages followed the ancient pattern, and so precisely, what about the last?"

"As long as Israel continued its descent from God, the progression had to continue, so too with America."

"The progression of judgment."

"The progression of warnings and judgment."

"So that's what lies ahead," I asked, "warnings and judgment?"

"And periods of grace and relief."

"As in the years after 9/11."

"Yes, and just as in that period, the progression continues, visible or invisible, above the surface or beneath it. And the voice of God continues to call."

"And if the nation doesn't listen?" I asked.

"Then there comes calamity. From the commentaries on Isaiah 9:

> "That which God designs, in smiting us, is to turn us to himself and to set us a seeking him; *and, if this point be not gained by lesser judgments, greater may be expected...*"[1]

"Calamities," I said, "taking the form of what?"

"They may take the form of economic disintegration or military defeat, disorder and division, the collapse of infrastructure, man-made calamities, calamities of nature, decline and fall. And, in the case of a nation so greatly blessed by God's favor, the withdrawal of all such blessings."

"Prosperity, protection, peace."

"Yes. And in the case of a nation preeminent among the nations, it means the end of that preeminence...the collapse of empire...the removing of its crown."

"Was 9/11 a shadow then?" I asked.

"As 9/11 was a day of symbol. The World Trade Center was a symbol of what?"

"America's financial power, America's global economic preeminence."

"And so its fall," he said. "Of what would that speak?"

"It would foretell the fall of America's financial economic power."

"Yes," said the prophet, "the fall of the American empire, the end of the American age, warned of and foreshadowed by 9/11, and after its pattern...just as the vow of Isaiah 9:10 bears its fruit as in the next verse."

"Isaiah 9:11."

"Do you remember what it said?"

"You'll have to refresh my memory."

"It said this:

> "Therefore the LORD shall set up
> The adversaries of Rezin against him,
> And spur his enemies on.[2]

"It's the beginning of destruction. It goes on:

> "And they shall devour Israel with an open mouth.
> For all this His anger is not turned away,
> But His hand is stretched out still....
> The land is burned up....
> What will you do in the day of punishment,
> And in the desolation which will come from afar?
> To whom will you flee for help?[3]

"So what is it saying?" asked the prophet.

"It's a prophecy of national destruction," I replied. "Isaiah 9:10 leads into a prophecy of national destruction."

"As the words of the vow of Isaiah 9:10 would actually usher in that destruction."

"How?"

"The same spirit of defiance, first given voice in that vow, would ultimately lead the nation into a fatal mistake. It would rise up in defiance of the Assyrian Empire. That defiance, in turn, would lead the Assyrians to invade the land once more, but this time not as a warning."

"But to destroy it."

"They would be under siege three years. Then, in the year 722 B.C., their defenses would collapse, and the kingdom of Israel would vanish from the pages of history."

"So that whole first attack of fallen bricks and sycamores would end up being a harbinger of an even greater judgment."

"A warning and a harbinger."

"But did that which *was* to come," I asked, "*have* to come?"

"A paradox," he answered.

"Was it irrevocable? Is it possible that God could have been merciful instead?"

"Merciful instead? Nouriel, do you still not understand Him? God's will is that none should perish. Judgment isn't His desire...but His necessity. The good must bring evil to an end, or else it would cease to be good. And yet His mercy is still greater than judgment. His heart always wills for redemption. And therein lies the hope."

"The hope for America?" I asked.

"Sodom was a city of corruption and violence, immorality, depravity. Yet there was still hope. God would have spared the entire city if only ten righteous people could have been found within it."

"But Sodom was destroyed."

"Because," he said, "it didn't even have ten. Then there was the kingdom of Judah, a kingdom that had once known God and yet had now fallen so low that the land was filled with altars to foreign gods, covered with the blood of its children. Its judgment was decreed. But then a righteous man named Josiah ascended the throne. King Josiah attempted to reverse Israel's spiritual descent. He banned the pagan practices, destroyed the idols, smashed the altars, and sought to restore the nation to God."

"So then the judgment *didn't* come?" I asked.

"No," he replied, "the judgment *did* come."

"But I thought..."

"It came because the nation never fully changed its course, and, after Josiah's death, it resumed its spiritual descent. But as long as Josiah lived, the judgment was forestalled."

"So judgment can be delayed."

"Yes, even for the sake of one man. And then there was Nineveh, the great Assyrian city."

"As in the Assyrian Empire?"

"As in the merciless, arrogant, brutal, cold-blooded Assyrian empire. Its judgment was also decreed. God called the prophet Jonah to go there and proclaim the coming destruction. But Jonah did everything he could to avoid answering his call."

"Because he didn't want to proclaim their judgment?"

"No," said the prophet, "because he didn't want them to be saved. He knew that God's will was not for judgment but mercy."

"But he ended up going there."

"After some persuasion."

"And..."

"The people of Nineveh received the prophetic warning

given them. The call went forth from the leaders to all the city's inhabitants, to repent, to pray, and to seek God's mercy."

"And..."

"And God heard their prayers. And the judgment was turned away."

"But if their judgment was decreed and proclaimed," I asked, "how could it not happen?"

"What should concern us more, Nouriel, that the judgment didn't happen as proclaimed or that thousands of lives were saved? You see, the one who wills for judgment is man, not God. The heart of God wills for salvation. Greater than His judgments are His compassions."

"How long," I asked, "was it from Isaiah 9:10 to the nation's judgment, or from the time of the first Assyrian invasion to the destruction of Israel?"

"About ten years," he replied.

"And what about the southern kingdom, Judah, did it follow the same pattern—an initial attack, a harbinger, and then destruction?"

"Yes, the same pattern. First came the initial invasion in 605 B.C., this time by the Babylonians. Later, the same army would return to destroy the land, the city, and the Temple."

"When?" I asked.

"586 B.C."

"So from the time of the first incursion to the time of the destruction...about twenty years."

"Yes. But there's no formula," he replied. "Each case is different."

"But there's a pattern."

"A pattern, yes, but each case is different."

"So Israel is warned but doesn't turn back and is destroyed. Sodom could have been saved for the sake of ten righteous people, but there weren't even ten, and the city was destroyed. The judgment of Judah is decreed but held back, averted for a set time, because of one righteous king. And Nineveh is told of its judgment by a prophet who doesn't even want the city to repent, but they repent nevertheless and their judgment is turned away."

"Correct."

"So which of these is the case of America?"

"America is its *own* case," he said. "As long as we have breath and as long as God is merciful, there's hope. But the nation's hope is dependent."

"On..."

"Its response to God's calling."

"And God is still calling America?"

"Yes."

"And the message is..."

"You already know the message."

"The smiles of heaven cannot remain on a nation that disregards the ways of God. If America turns away from God, its blessings will likewise be removed and replaced with judgment."

"Not *if*," said the prophet.

"Not if?" I asked.

"Not *if* America turns away from God," he said. "It's already turning. So what then is the message?"

"Return?"

"Yes," said the prophet. "The message is *return*."

"But how does a nation return to God?"

"You never read the message on the paper."

"In my dream?"

"In your dream."

"No. I woke up. But it was Washington's message, the warning for a nation that disregards the eternal rules of heaven."

"Yes," he replied, "that's part of the message. But in your dream, it wasn't just Washington. Washington and King Solomon were joined together."

"So?"

"So the message is twofold. There's another part to it, another prophetic word, and this time from King Solomon."

"From King Solomon to America?"

"For that nation that has turned from God, for that nation from which the smiles of heaven have been withdrawn."

"And this word came during the dedication of the Temple?" I asked.

"It came when the dedication was finished," he replied. "God appeared to Solomon in the night to give him a word, an answer to the prayers he prayed on the Temple Mount."

"The prayers he prayed over the nation's future...for the day of its fall from God and the calamity it would suffer as a result."

"Yes. And now God was giving Solomon the answer to his prayer and the answer for a nation under the shadow of judgment. This is the message *now for America*."

The prophet then handed me a Bible, a little black Bible, small enough to fit into someone's shirt pocket.

"Open it up," he said, "to the Book of 2 Chronicles, chapter 7, verse 14. And read it."

So I opened it and read the words out loud:

> If My people who are called by My name will humble themselves, and pray and seek My face, and turn from their wicked ways, then I will hear from heaven, and will forgive their sin and heal their land.[4]

"That's the word, Nouriel. That's the word appointed for America."

"*If My people*," I said. "And who are '*My people*'?"

"As given to Solomon, *My people* would refer to the nation as a whole, and, more specifically, those within the nation who could genuinely be called the people of God, those who followed His ways."

"And what would it mean applied now to America?"

"It's the call of God to a nation once dedicated to His purposes but now falling away from His will. It's the call of God to return."

"And a call to those who follow His ways...to believers?"

"Exactly."

"But why would believers have to return?" I asked.

"The call of repentance is for the righteous and unrighteous, the godly and ungodly alike. If the righteous had been the lights they were called to be, the nation would never have fallen as it did."

"In Israel or America?"

"Both."

"*Will humble themselves…* An entire nation humbling itself?"

"As Nineveh did, and was saved."

"*And pray and seek My face.*"

"America was founded on prayer. Therefore the removal of prayer from its public life was a central part of its fall from God. A nation that turns away from prayer will ultimately find itself in desperate need of it. The calamity returned America to the ground of its consecration—the nation was being called to return to God in prayer."

"But didn't it already happen in a sense? After 9/11, the nation's houses of worship were filled with people."

"A momentary seeking for comfort in the face of calamity has nothing to do with the prayer and change needed to turn away a nation's judgment—just as saying *God bless America* has nothing to do with seeking His face."

"And how does one seek His face?" I asked.

"First, by taking it seriously enough to turn away from everything else, from every other pursuit."

"*And turn from their wicked ways.*"

"Yes," said the prophet, "the crux of the matter—repentance. With all the talk of God blessing America in the wake of 9/11, the great missing factor was repentance. Without that, everything else is null and void. America must face the magnitude of its moral and spiritual descent, the degrading of its culture… to the multitude of its idols… to its fall into ever deeper immoralities."

"The idols of…"

"Carnality, impurity, greed, materialism, vanity, self-obsession… and the altars covered with the blood of its innocent. Without a change of course, there can be no change of destination. Only in repentance can judgment be averted, and only in a true turning away from darkness to the light."

"And what about those called by His name," I asked, "the believers? They also need to repent?"

"They need to be the *first* to repent."

"From what?"

"From their apathy, from their complacency...their com-promises with darkness...their omissions...their serving of other gods...their sins committed in secret...their withholding of life...and their failure to fulfill their call."

"Their call?"

"To be the light of the world."

"And if there *is* a turning?" I asked.

"Then He *will* hear from heaven and forgive their sins and heal their land.'"

"And that's a certainty?"

"His part is a certainty. His love is a certainty. His mercy is a certainty. His arms are open. His mercy is without end. And there's no sin so deep that His love is not deeper still."

"So which will it be for America," I asked, "judgment or redemption?"

"The matter of the end..." he said.

"What will the end be?" I asked again. "Judgment or redemption?"

"Or redemption born in judgment," he replied. "What does the future hold? What lies in store for America? Three words, Nouriel...it all rests on three words: *If My people!*"

"A nation's future resting on three words."

"Even just one," said the prophet.

"The nation's future resting on one word..."

"*If.*"

◆◆◆

"Our time is almost up," he said.

"The time of our encounter?"

"Our time together, the time of impartation. We've come to the end of the matter."

"The matter?"

"The matter of the end."

"Then what's left?" I asked.

"That which comes after."

"After the end?"

"After the end."

"How could anything come after the end?" I asked. "If it could, the end wouldn't be the end."

"Then perhaps it's not."

"But then..."

"Come."

Chapter 21

Eternity

א ה

H E LED ME away from Ground Zero to the water's edge, which was a short walk."

"So you were on the west side," said Ana, "by the Hudson, just as you were the first time you saw him."

"By the Hudson," he replied, "except when I first saw him, we were much farther up."

"And this was the lower west side, of course. Was there anything significant that he wanted you to see?"

"No. I think he just wanted to take me away from everything else, from any distraction. It was now late afternoon. The water was shimmering with golden light. In view of the setting, his question didn't seem to fit."

◆◆◆

"And what will you do on the Day of Judgment?" he asked.

"You definitely know how to ruin a moment," I replied. "What will I do?"

"'*What will you do on the day of judgment...the day of punishment*?' The words are from the prophecy. It's what Isaiah 9:10 leads up to. It's what the Lord asked the people of Israel before the final calamity."

"It's a daunting question, and a scary predicament to be living then...in view of everything that was coming."

"And what if it *were* you, Nouriel, living there at that time, walking in their sandals? What if it were you who heard the voice of the prophets, and understood the Harbingers, and knew the judgment was coming? Everyone around you was oblivious to it.

226

Everyone just went on with their lives with no idea of what was coming. What would you do?"

"I'd want them to know. I'd want them to be saved. I'd tell them."

"But who would listen to you? Who would take your warning seriously? And what about your own predicament? A nation's heading for judgment, but you're part of it. How do you save yourself? What will *you* do on the Day of Judgment? Where will you go to find safety?"

"Outside the country, I guess."

"Judgment isn't a matter of geography. It doesn't matter where you are. No place is far enough away, and no refuge strong enough."

"So what would I do?"

"The reason I ask is because you *do* live in such a time and place, and you *have* heard the voice of the prophets, and you *do* understand the Harbingers and know what they portend. So the question isn't hypothetical. And it's not even, 'What *would* you do?' What *will* you do? What will you do, Nouriel, on the Day of Judgment?"

"On the day of a nation's judgment?"

"On the day of *your* judgment," said the prophet. "What if you were one of them, back then, and your life ended before the nation's judgment came? What then?"

"What then?"

"Would you then have escaped judgment?"

"Yes," I replied.

"No. You wouldn't. Judgment isn't ultimately about nations—but people. As it's written: *'It's appointed for man once to die and then judgment.'* After the end comes the Day of Judgment, in light of which all other judgments are only foreshadows. And no one is exempt. Each must stand before Him."

"Why?"

"Why judgment?"

"Yes."

"It must be. As long as there's evil, there has to be judgment. Every sin, every wrong, every evil has to be brought to an end. Without it, there would be no hope."

"Without judgment there would be no hope?" I asked.

"Without judgment, there would be no end to evil in the universe...or in man's heart. There would be no heaven."

"Why would there be no heaven?"

He looked away from me and toward the light of the setting sun before speaking again. "Because heaven would then be filled with locks and prisons, hatred, violence, fear, and destruction. Heaven would cease to be heaven...and would become hell instead. But there *is* a heaven, and there is a time and place of no more sorrow...no more hate...no more weeping or tears...and no more pain. There must be a judgment. Evil must end...beyond which is heaven."

"So, in other words, if evil entered heaven, heaven would cease to be heaven because it would have evil in it."

"Yes," he answered. "And who is evil?"

"Those who kill, who deceive, who steal, those who hurt and abuse others..."

"And that's it?" he asked.

"I'm sure there are other categories."

"And what about you, Nouriel? Do you fit into any of those categories?"

"No."

"No," he replied, "you wouldn't. But remember, '*All the ways of a man are right in his own eyes.*' It's from the Book of Proverbs. That's human nature. So be careful of the image that appears in your own eyes. Beware of the good Nazi."

"The good Nazi? And what's that supposed to mean?"

"The Nazis sent millions to their deaths out of pure hatred and evil. Can you think of a people more evil than that? And yet do you think most of them saw themselves as evil?"

"No."

"And why not?" he asked. "Because they compared themselves and measured themselves by the standards they themselves created. Each, in his own eyes, was a good Nazi, a moral Nazi, a decent Nazi, a religious Nazi, and a Nazi no worse than the next. For by seeing themselves in their own eyes, they became blind. But their judgment would come in the form of destruction, and their sins would be exposed before the world."

"But there's a big difference between the Nazis and most people."

"The principle is the same. You can never judge yourself by your own standards and your own righteousness, but only in light of *His* righteousness."

"And how do we hold up in the light of His righteousness?"

"Which do you think is greater," he asked, "the moral distance that separates us from the most monstrous of Nazis or that which separates us from God?"

"I guess that which separates us from God."

"That's correct, because the first separation is finite. But the second is infinite. So what we see as the slightest of sins within ourselves appears, in the eyes of Him who is absolute goodness, even more abhorrently evil than the crimes of the Nazis appear to us. In the light of the absolute Good, our lust becomes as adultery and our hatred as murder."

"But then who could stand?" I asked. "Who could make it into heaven?"

"No one could stand, and no one could make it into heaven. How far would just one sin take you away from the infinite righteousness of God?"

"An infinite distance?"

"Yes. So how far are we from heaven?"

"An infinite distance."

"And how great is the judgment?"

"Infinitely great."

"And how long would it take us to bridge the gap, to be reconciled to God, to enter heaven?"

"An infinity of time."

"Eternity," he said.

"So we could never get there, could we?"

"And to be infinitely separated from God and heaven...is what?" he asked.

"Hell?"

"Hell—infinite separation from God and from all things good; total, infinite, eternal judgment."

"We don't just die?"

"The soul is eternal," he said. "One way or another, at the end of a thousand ages, you'll still exist. The question is *where*. And if the joy and glory of being in God's presence in heaven is beyond our imagining, so then too is the darkness and horror of being in His absence...without Him forever...hell."

"So then our predicament is even more grave than that of a nation in its hour of judgment."

"The prospect of entering eternity without God, on the wrong side of an infinite judgment, is far graver than the judgment of any nation—infinitely more so. Nations are temporary; the soul is eternal. So, Nouriel, I'm asking you again, what will you do on the Day of Judgment?"

"Tell me."

"If you have an infinite gap and an infinite problem, what do you need?"

"An infinite answer?"

"Which means that the answer could not come from yourself or from this world. It could only come from the infinite, from heaven...from God, which means that any given answer, any given ideology, and any given system based on the efforts of man is ruled out."

"Which rules out most answers," I said.

"Which rules out *every* answer," he replied, "every answer based on man trying to reach God, a hand reaching upward to heaven. The answer can only come the other way, from the infinite to the finite, from heaven to earth...from God to man."

"A hand reaching down from heaven?"

"Exactly. And what alone could answer an infinite judgment?"

"An infinite mercy?"

"Yes, the infinite mercy of an infinite love. And what alone could fill an infinite absence?"

"An infinite presence."

"The infinite presence of the infinite love."

He paused after saying that and turned away from the sun and the water so that he was looking directly into my eyes when he spoke again.

"Nouriel, did you know that there's a part of the World Trade Center that still stands?"

"No, I never heard that."

"A part of the World Trade Center stands to this day, in this city."

"It stands in what way?" I asked.

"As a sign," he replied, "literally."

"I don't understand."

"On the third day after the calamity, a construction worker was standing in the ruins of one of the shattered buildings. When he looked up, he saw it."

"The sign…"

"The sign…unmistakable…glaring…forged not by human hands but by the force of the calamity…a cross…a perfectly formed cross…twenty feet high…of cast iron beams from the fallen towers standing in the midst of a landscape of devastation…as if rising up from the ruins. When he saw it, he couldn't hold back from weeping. In the days and weeks that followed, it would become known as *the Cross of Ground Zero*, a sign of faith and hope in the midst of the calamity, a sign again calling to a nation to return. But not only to a nation…a sign calling each to return."

"Is that the answer you spoke of?"

"The answer to judgment. For what alone is it that can answer an infinite judgment and bridge an infinite chasm?

"An infinite love," I said. "The infinite presence of an infinite love."

"Of the infinite One," he said.

"You mean God."

"God."

"But you haven't mentioned the word *religion* even once."

"Because it's not about religion; it's about love. That's the meaning of the sign, the overcoming of the infinite judgment by the infinite love."

"The love of God."

"The love of God. For God is love, and the nature of love is what?"

"To give?" I replied.

"Yes, to give of itself, to put itself in the place of the other even if it means that by so doing it must sacrifice itself. So if God is love, then what would the ultimate manifestation of love be?"

"I don't know."

"The giving of Himself…God giving Himself to bear the judgment of those under judgment if, by so doing, it would save them. Love puts itself in the place of the other. So then the ultimate manifestation of love would be…"

"God putting Himself in our place."

"In our life, in our death, in our judgment…the sacrifice."

"As in Jesus…"

"The infinite sacrifice," said the prophet, "to bear an infinite judgment, in which all sins are nullified and all who partake are set free…forgiven…saved. An infinite redemption in which judgment and death are overcome and a new life given…a new beginning…a new birth. The love of God is greater than judgment….Remember…there is no sin so deep that His love isn't deeper…and no life so hopeless…no soul so far away…and no darkness so dark that His love isn't greater still."

"But this is all…I wasn't born with it, or raised in it, and I'm not religious."

"Being religious has nothing to do with it," he said. "There's no religion in heaven, only love. It's the heart, Nouriel. And you couldn't have been born into it to begin with, only born *again* into it. And it can't happen without you choosing it."

"To be born again?"

"Yes. Do you know His real name?"

"Jesus?"

"Yes."

"I thought that *was* His real name."

"His real name is *Yeshua*. It's Hebrew. He was Jewish, as were all His disciples, and the message they proclaimed was all about the Jewish Messiah, the fulfillment of the Hebrew Scriptures, the Hope of Israel. *Yeshua* is Hebrew for *God is Salvation*, or *God is*

Deliverance...Protection...Rescue...Freedom...Refuge... and *Safety.* In the Day of Judgment, there's no safe ground...no salvation, except in Him who *is* salvation."

"So how does one become saved?"

"*'You cannot see the kingdom of God unless you are born again.'* Those are *His* words."

"And how does one become born again?"

"By receiving...by letting go...by letting the old life end and a new one begin. By choosing...by opening your heart to receive that which is beyond containing—the presence...the mercy...the forgiveness...the cleansing...the unending love of God."

"By receiving what exactly?"

"The gift, freely given and freely received, and yet so great a gift that you treasure it above life itself...so great a gift that it changes everything else."

"And the gift is..."

"If God is love, and love is a gift, then the Giver and the Gift are one."

"Then the gift is God?"

"Salvation comes in the *giving* of His life and is complete in the *receiving* of His life. Think of a bride and a bridegroom."

"A bride and bridegroom?"

"The bridegroom gives everything he has for the bride, even his life. The bride must do likewise. He calls her. If she says yes, everything he has becomes hers, and everything she has becomes his. Her burdens become his burdens, her sins become his sins. He becomes hers, and she becomes his. She leaves her old life behind for a new one, to go with her beloved. Wherever he goes, she goes with him, and wherever she dwells, he never leaves her. He loves her with all his being, as she loves him. The one lives for the other, and the other for the one. The two become as one."

"So the bridegroom is..."

"God."

"And the bride is..."

"The one who receives him."

"Sounds beautiful," I said.

"It *is* beautiful…the most beautiful thing you could possibly find or ever know or ever have in your days on earth."

"It's a love story."

"After all is said and done, that's what it was always meant to be…a love story."

"A marriage."

"Yes, an eternal marriage for which we were all born, and of which no one was to be left out, that no one would enter eternity alone."

"And it begins…"

"It begins with the receiving…with the opening of one's heart…with the turning away from darkness and to the light…with the giving of oneself…the committing of one's life—a vow of love…a prayer…decision…a total and unconditional *yes*."

"And it takes place…"

"Anywhere, any place, alone or with others, wherever you are. It takes place anywhere, for it takes place in the heart."

"And at any time?"

"No, Nouriel," he said. "It doesn't take place at any time. It only takes place at *one* time."

"What *one* time?"

"*Now…*" said the prophet. "Now is the only time in which it can happen. As it is written, '*Now is the time of salvation*,' never tomorrow, only now."

"But if we were talking tomorrow, it could still happen then."

"Yes, but only when then has become now, and tomorrow is today. But when it does, you may not be there."

"And why wouldn't I be?"

"How far away from eternity do you think you are, Nouriel?"

"How could I possibly know that?"

"But you can know that," he replied.

"Then what's the answer?" I asked. "How far am I away from eternity?"

"One heartbeat," he replied, "one heartbeat. That's it. That's all. You're only one heartbeat away from eternity. Everything you have—your life, your breath, this moment, it's all borrowed, it's all a gift. And at any moment it all ends with a heartbeat…just one heartbeat, and there's no more time. One heartbeat and the chance to be saved is gone. One heartbeat and there's no more choosing— it's all sealed for eternal life or eternal death."

"But if I didn't choose…"

"Then you already have. If you don't choose to be saved, then you've chosen not to be saved. Your life and your eternity…it all rests on one heartbeat. *And what will you do on the Day of Judgment?* Remember the question, Nouriel…because in the end it's the only question. Remember the question…because no one knows when that day will come. The only thing you can be sure of is that it *will* come, and the only time you can be sure of is now. Now is all you have. And now is the time of salvation."

"It's too big a decision to make just like that."

"It's too big a decision *not* to," he said.

"I would have to see to believe."

"No, Nouriel, you have to *believe* in order to see and to find what you're searching for."

"And what is it that I'm searching for?"

"The meaning, the purpose of your life, the reason you were born. It's the only way you can ever find it.…Only in Him who gave you life, can you find its meaning."

"I need time."

"And you have it, Nouriel…up until the last heartbeat."

◆◆◆

He allowed a few moments of silence to let his words sink in as I stared into the distant waters.

"The seal," he said. "May I have it back?"

So I returned it to him.

"And with this," said the prophet, "it's finished. The time of the revealing of mysteries is complete."

"So then you don't have anything more to give me?" I asked.

He paused and looked at me with the look of a shopkeeper when asked for an item he no longer has in stock. But then his expression changed. "Come to think of it," he said, "I do."

"There's another seal?"

"Yes, come to think of it." He reached into his coat pocket, took it out, and handed it to me.

———————◆◆◆———————

"What was it?" she asked.

"It was the first one, the very first seal."

"Wait, I thought he just gave you the first seal, the seal of the First Harbinger, and you gave it back to him."

"No. There was another. There was another before that seal. The seal I gave *him* at the beginning."

"The one that came in the mail?" she asked.

"Yes, the one that started everything. I hadn't seen it since the day I gave it away, years before, when it all began."

———————◆◆◆———————

"It's only right that it be returned to its owner," he said. "It's *your* seal, your security deposit. You see? I gave you my word you'd get it back."

"You told me I'd get it back when we were finished with the Harbingers."

"So then we are."

"And there's nothing more?"

"More?"

"No more mysteries, no more revelations?"

"You have all you need now."

"So then…"

"So then," he said, "this is it."

"So…"

"So it's time for us to part."

"That's it?"

"Good-bye, Nouriel."

But this time he didn't leave. He remained by the waters as if waiting for me to go first. So I began walking away, finding it hard to accept the finality of it all. It was about ten seconds into my departure that I heard his voice.

"Oh," he said, "there *is* something."

I froze in place, and without turning back, but looking straight ahead, I responded. "What?" I asked.

"You never answered my question."

"*I* never answered *your* question? And what question was that?"

"*Why were you given the seal?* I asked you that at the beginning, but you never gave me an answer."

"And why would you need to know the answer to that?"

"I don't."

"Then why do you ask the question?"

"Because *you* do."

"*I* do?"

"Yes. You're the one who needs to know the answer to the question."

"Then why am I not asking it?"

"That's a good question."

"A good question why I'm not asking the question?"

"Yes," he said. "It is a mystery."

"A mystery to *you*?"

"Yes."

"That's a switch."

"Why were you given the seal?"

"Is that another mystery?" I asked. "Is this the last mystery?"

"Answer the question, Nouriel...and you'll know."

Chapter 22

The Last Seal

אח

S O WHAT HAPPENED?" she asked.
"Nothing at first, nothing revealing why I was given the seal. There was another matter, more pressing, that I had to deal with."

"More pressing?"

"The matter of eternity. It haunted my thoughts. It was the one thing on which everything else stood or fell. If I didn't get that part right, the rest wouldn't matter, my life, everything. Everything would come to an end, and then...eternity. Everything would end with eternity—the one thing that wouldn't end, the only thing that would be left when everything else was gone...and so the only thing that would matter. I had to get that part right. I had to get my life right with God."

"And did you?"

"Yes."

"How?"

"By following his words."

"And what happened?"

"Everything began to change, not so much around me, not my circumstances, but within. It was a release, a completion, and, for the first time in my life, I had a real peace."

"And what happened after that?"

"After that, I tried to make sense of everything that happened up to that point—my encounters with the prophet, everything that was shown to me, all the revelations of the mysteries. I had no idea what I was supposed to do with it. And why me? I tried to go on with my life as normal, as I had before the prophet, before the Harbingers, before receiving that envelope. I tried...but it was impossible. I was a writer of articles, the purpose of which being to entertain my readers or, at best, to provoke them. But in light of the revelations, everything I was doing now seemed irredeemably shallow and trivial, of no consequence. And then there was the burden."

"The burden?"

"Of what I knew."

"You were burdened about the future?"

"Not for myself," he said. "I wasn't afraid for myself, but for others. The veil had been removed so I could see, so I could be warned. But what about everyone else? They had no idea. They had no clue of what was happening or where it was all heading."

"Sounds like what the prophets must have gone through," she said.

"I couldn't escape it. And yet there was nothing I could do about it…a burden with no direction. I took out the seal."

"The last seal."

"And the first…to go over it in detail."

"You never did that before?" she asked.

"Not seriously…not as seriously as I had with the others. When I first received it, I had no assurance that there was any meaning to it. And when he returned it, at the end, there didn't seem to be any reason to. The mysteries were finished except for why I was the one given them in the first place. And it wasn't like the other seals. It didn't have an image, just ancient-looking inscriptions. Its purpose, I assumed, was to begin the search, and then to end it. I didn't think there was much left to discover now that it was all over."

"And was there?"

"The writing on the seal was in a language I had never seen before. But I remembered the words of the prophet that day we first met on the bench, when he took the seal to examine it. He said it was Hebrew, but a different form of Hebrew—Paleo-Hebrew, an older version."

"And did you know anybody who could read Paleo-Hebrew?"

"No. But I knew someone who studied Hebrew from biblical and rabbinical writings. I looked up the Paleo-Hebrew alphabet, then transcribed each of the letters into its modern Hebrew equivalent. Then I made a trip to Brooklyn. That's where my friend was, an Orthodox Jewish man who ran a little bookstore, in back of which was a study, a library of all sorts of mystical Hebrew writings. That was his passion—finding meaning in mystical Hebrew literature. I figured he'd be the right one. When I told him the purpose of my coming, he closed up the shop and led me to the back room. We sat down at a bare wooden table surrounded by bookcases. He put on his reading glasses and began examining the transcription. After a few moments of silence, he began deciphering it:

"'*Baruch*,' he said. 'It means, *blessed*. It's the word that begins most Hebrew prayers.

"'*Yahu* or *Yah*. It's the sacred name of God, so sacred I shouldn't be saying it, but so I did. So, *Blessed of God*.

"'*Ben*.—It means, *the son*. *Blessed of God is the son*.

"'*Neri* means *light* and *Yahu*, again, the name of God. So *the light of God*.

"'*Ha Sofer*, '*the one who declares* or *the declarer*.'

"'So what is it saying?' I asked."

"'It's saying: "*Blessed of God is the son of the Light of God, the declarer*."'

"'And what is that supposed to mean?' I asked.

"'How should I know?' he replied. 'You're the one who gave it to me.'

"'But what do you think it means?'

"'It sounds like a blessing for a righteous man, a child of the light.'

"'And *the declarer*...the declarer of what?'

"'How I should know the declarer of what?'

"'Have you ever come across anything like that before in your studies?

"'I've come across many Hebrew blessings, but I don't remember anything quite like this. You copied it from an inscription?'

"'Yes.'

"'Maybe from an amulet or something?'

"'Something.'"

"'An inscription with a Hebrew blessing is not such a strange thing. It's a blessing. So you have a blessing.'

"'But what does it mean?'

"'It means you're a blessed man.'

"And that's all he gave me."

"So what did you make of it?" she asked.

"I didn't know what to make of it. The translation really didn't give me anything to go on. It didn't seem to have anything to do with anything."

"But now you knew what the inscription meant."

"Yes. Now I knew what it meant and had no idea what it signified."

"So what did you do?"

"I went for a walk along the Hudson. It was a cloudy, windy day. It was late afternoon. Halfway into the walk I decided to take a break. There was an empty bench nearby. It was, though I didn't realize it at the time, the same bench on which the prophet was sitting when we first met. I sat down, took out the seal, and just stared at it as I pondered my lack of direction and my still unresolved burden. I was lost in thought for several minutes before I heard a voice from behind.

"'Looks like a storm.'"

"The same words," she said. "The same words the prophet spoke to you at the very beginning."

"The same words and the same voice."

—————◆◆◆—————

"It does," I answered, without breaking my gaze, without turning around to see who was speaking.

"What's that," he asked, "in your hand? Some archaeological artifact?"

"One of several," I said, "each with a mystery."

"And this one? Of what mystery does it speak?" he asked.

"I don't know. It speaks...but it doesn't say anything...nothing that means anything."

"So you haven't figured it out yet?"

"I know what it says, but I don't know what it means."

With that, the prophet came around to the front of the bench. "Still?" he asked.

"Still," I answered.

He sat down. "It all began with that seal," he said, "and right here."

"But I still don't know what it means or what I'm supposed to do with it all."

"But you said you knew what it says."

"Yes."

"So tell me what it says."

"*Blessed of God is the son of God's light, the declarer.*"

"Who told you it said that?"

"A friend...a friend who specializes in mystical Hebrew writings."

"Did you ever look in a mirror," he asked, "and not realize that the man staring back at you was your own reflection?"

"I don't know...maybe. Why?"

"Because you're doing it now."

"What do you mean?"

"It's possible to become too mystical and miss the obvious."

"Then that's not what it says."

"If you took it piece by piece and with no context, it could be understood to mean that. But that's not what it says."

"Then what?"

"What your friend translated as *Blessed of God* is the Hebrew *Baruchyahu* from the Hebrew *baruch, blessed*, and *Yahu*, the Lord."

"But that's almost the same thing."

"But it's not a blessing. It's not even a sentence."

"Then what it is it?" I asked.

"It's a name."

"A name?"

"The name of a person...a person named *Baruch*."

"Baruch."

"And what your friend translated as *the son* is the Hebrew word *ben*, which, in this case, is part of the name, '*Baruch, son of...*'"

"*Ben...Son of...*I should have known that."

"And what he translated as *God's light* is the Hebrew *Neriyahu*' or '*Neriah—the light of God*, yes, but it's also a name, *Neriah*. Neriah was Baruch's father...*Baruch ben Neriah*."

"Baruch, son of Neriah. So who *was* he?"

"Think of the seals, Nouriel. What was their purpose?"

"To seal or authenticate an important message."

"And who used them?" he asked.

"Kings, leaders, government officials."

"And who else?"

"I don't know."

"And scribes. Scribes used them because it was they who wrote the messages. After the name is a title: *Ha Sofer.*"

"*The one who declares.*"

"Yes, it can mean that as well, *one who declares, who tells, who reveals*. But what it means on the seal is *the Scribe*."

"So Baruch was a scribe."

"Yes."

"And why is that significant?" I asked.

"Because Baruch is mentioned in the Bible, and because he wasn't just a scribe."

"What then?"

"He was the scribe of a particular prophet."

"Which prophet?"

"The prophet Jeremiah. Baruch was the one who wrote down Jeremiah's prophecies. Jeremiah would prophesy, and Baruch would commit the prophecy to writing. As it is written:

> "Then Jeremiah called Baruch the son of Neriah; and Baruch
> wrote on a scroll of a book, at the instruction of Jeremiah, all
> the words of the LORD which He had spoken to him."[1]

"So this is the seal of Baruch," I said. "The seal he used to authenticate his writings."

"It's one of them," said the prophet.

"I still don't get it."

"Still?"

"No."

"Then answer the question I asked you."

"Why I was given the seal?"

"Yes."

"Because a seal has to do with a message?"

"But why *you*?" he asked. "Why was the seal given to *you*?"

"I have no idea."

"What was Baruch?"

"A scribe."

"And what is a scribe?"

"One who writes."

"A writer...a scribe is a writer. And what are you, Nouriel?"

"A writer."

"A writer."

"What are you saying? I was chosen because I was a writer?"

"No," he said, "you weren't chosen because you were a writer. You were a writer, because you were chosen."

"And what's that supposed to mean?"

"It was the reason you became a writer in the first place. It was all for this purpose, all for this time."

"No. The reason I became a writer was because I..."

"No, Nouriel. *The Almighty has His own purposes.* And why do you think each revelation came to you through a seal? It's because of *you*. It's because of *your* calling. You're the *sofer*, the scribe, he who declares, who reveals. Do you know what that word also means?"

"No."

"*He who records.*"

"As in he who records on a scroll."

"Or, in the present case, he who records on a recording device."

"This is too..."

"The rabbis say that Baruch was born of the priestly line, as was Jeremiah."

"And...?"

"And what's your last name?"

"Kaplan."

"Kaplan, if I'm not mistaken, is a priestly name, isn't it?"

"It is."

"Indicating one who is born of the priestly line. So you too were born of the priestly line, and for this moment."

———— ◆◆◆ ————

"You must have been blown away," said Ana, "when he started telling you all this. It must have blown you away."

"I was...and it did...but it didn't stop there."

———— ◆◆◆ ————

"What's your name?" he asked.

"You know my name," I replied. "Why do you ask?

"What's your name?" he asked again.

"Nouriel."

"No. That's your middle name. That's what you used when you started writing. What's your first name?"

"Barry."

"That's what your friends called you. That's what you wanted them to call you because you weren't comfortable with your real name. Your real name wasn't Barry. What was the name you were given when you were born?"

I hesitated in responding, but there was no way to avoid it. It came out softly, almost under my breath.

"Baruch."

He was silent.

"My name," I said, in a voice still soft but louder than before, "is Baruch."

◆◆◆

"Baruch!" she exclaimed. "He knew it all along! It's as if you were chosen for it…even from your birth."

◆◆◆

"Your name," he said, "is *Baruch Nouriel*. The name of Jeremiah's scribe was *Baruch ben Neriah*—*Neriah* meaning, *the light of God* or *the flame of God*. Do you know what *Nouriel* means?"

"No."

"*Nouriel* means *the flame of God*. In effect, it's the same name."

"What are you saying?" I asked, my voice now shaking.

"*You*, Nouriel…you are the final mystery. You're the mystery looking in the mirror and not recognizing that the image is you."

"You're saying I'm him?"

"No, you're not him. You're you. But you have the same calling."

"Which is…?"

"The *sofer*," he said, "You're the *sofer*. The one called to record, to declare, to make known, to make a record of what you've seen and heard, to write down the prophetic word, to reveal the mysteries that they might hear it, that a nation might hear it, and that those who will listen could be saved."

"My dream…At the end, you entrusted me with the paper…with the message. You gave it to me. Is that what's happening now?"

"So it is."

"So I'm your Baruch," I said, "and you're my Jeremiah?"

"Something like that," he answered.

"And I'm to write it all down?"

"Yes, and more:

> "And Jeremiah commanded Baruch, saying, 'I am confined,
> I cannot go into the house of the LORD. You go, therefore,
> and read from the scroll which you have written at my
> instruction, the words of the LORD, in the hearing of the
> people in the LORD's house on the day of fasting. And you

shall also read them in the hearing of all Judah who come from their cities.'[2]

"Jeremiah's movements were restricted. He couldn't deliver his prophecy in public, not in person. So he sent Baruch in his place so that the prophecy would be proclaimed publicly to all. So Baruch wasn't only Jeremiah's scribe but also, at times, his representative, his voice."

"Why are you telling me this?"

"Because I too am restricted. So you must go and make known the message, to give them the warning and the hope. Take what you wrote down at my dictation, and let it be known. You are the *sofer*, the one who must make known."

———————— ◆◆◆ ————————

"He was appointing you," she said. "The prophet was appointing you."

"Yes."

"And so that's why you came to me?"

"Yes."

"Because the message must be committed to writing and, through that, made known."

"Yes."

"In the form of a book."

"Yes."

"A book…yes…that would be your scroll. The message has to become a book…a book revealing the mystery behind everything…behind the news…behind the economy…behind the collapse…behind world history…the future…an ancient mystery on which the future of a nation hangs…. This is big, Nouriel. It's beyond big; it has to get out. They have to hear it. Do you have any idea how you're going to go about writing it?"

"No. I've never attempted anything quite like this. That's why I came to you."

"It's so big…and deep…and critical. You have to do it in a way that they can hear it…in a way that the message can go out to as many people as possible…in a way they can grasp. You're the writer, but I know what I would do."

"What would you do?" he asked

"I would take the message and put in the form of a narrative."

"What do you mean?"

"A story," she replied. "Commit the message to writing, but communicate it in the form of a story…a narrative…have somebody telling it…a narration."

"But it's a prophetic message."

"The Bible uses stories…pictures and parables to communicate messages of divine truth, doesn't it? The point is to get the message out to as many people as possible. The story would be the vehicle, the vessel through which the message, the mysteries, the revelations, the prophetic word would go forth."

"But if it takes on the form of a narrative, they might not realize that the revelations are real."

"They'll realize it."

"And who would narrate it?" he asked.

"You," she replied. "You'd write it just the way you told me. You'd create a character who narrates the account to another, just as you narrated it to me. Alter the details, change the names, make everyone into characters."

"And what about the message itself—the prophetic word, the mysteries. How would all that be communicated?"

"Reveal it in the same way it was revealed to you…by the prophet. Put it all into the form of conversations, as they were to begin with, between the one character and the other. You recorded everything. It's all there. Use what you already have. Transcribe the recordings. Let the prophet speak for himself, through his own words to you. And the message will get through."

"I don't know," he said. "I'll have to think about it."

"I wouldn't take too long," she replied.

"No."

"Why don't you ask the prophet?"

"I haven't seen him since that day."

"No?"

"No."

"Before you parted, did he give you any last words of counsel or guidance?"

"I guess you could call it that."

"And what was it?"

"At the very end of that last encounter, he led me over toward the water. The wind was now gusting wildly. There was definitely a storm coming."

◆◆◆

"So, Nouriel," he said, "do you think you're ready?"

"Ready?"

"To fulfill your call."

"I don't know, and I have no idea what to do."

"You'll be led, just as you were led to me."

"But it's not even my message. It's *your* message. I'd just be a messenger, a go-between. If they asked me anything about it, I wouldn't know what to say."

"No," he replied, "the message isn't mine. All I am is a messenger, as will be you."

"And if I needed help, would you be there?" I asked. "And how could I reach you?"

"I think you know better than that," he replied. "You don't need to reach me. The time of imparting is finished."

"So I won't see you again?"

"Unless He deems otherwise, no, you won't see me again."

The words hit me harder than I would have expected them to.

"You know," I said, "I think I'm going to miss our meetings…and all the uncertainty."

"The uncertainty?"

"Of not knowing when or where or how you'd appear next, and how it would happen to happen that I'd be there when you did."

"Things will still happen to happen," he said, "as you follow His leading."

"Still, I don't feel adequate, not remotely adequate for anything like this."

"How do you think Moses felt when he was called, or Jeremiah...or Mary...or Peter? Do you think any of them felt remotely adequate? It wasn't about them. And it's not about you. It's about Him. All you have to do is go where He sends you." Then he reached into his coat and took out a little horn...a little ram's horn. "Close your eyes, Nouriel," he said, lifting the horn above my head.

So I did. I soon felt a thick liquid rolling down my forehead.

◆◆◆

"It was oil?" she asked.

"Yes, I think olive oil."

"A horn of oil."

"The oil of anointing. It was when I felt it running down my cheeks that the prophet began to pray."

◆◆◆

"You," he said, "who are above all that is spoken and all that is named...

"I commit into Your hands Your servant. In his weakness, be to him a strength. In his not knowing, be to him his assurance. Cause him to walk in the footsteps You've prepared beforehand. Pour out upon him the Spirit of Your anointing that he might fulfill Your charge. Guide him. Protect him. Prepare his hands for battle. Bless and keep him. Cause the light of Your countenance to shine upon him. Spread over his life the tabernacle of Your glory, and shelter him in the covering of Your grace, in the name of the Anointed One, the Glory of Israel, the Light of the World."

I opened my eyes. The horn was gone. Looking into my eyes with what seemed to be a deep compassion tempered with what I took to be a sadness over our parting, he said, "God be with you, Baruch Nouriel."

"And God be with you," I replied.

And with that, he left. This time I stayed where I was.

"And I *still* didn't get your name," I shouted as he walked away.

"That's because I never gave it to you," he replied. Then he stopped walking and turned around. "You're still concerned," he said, in a gentle voice.

"The message," I said. "It's not exactly the kind that wins popularity contests, is it?"

"That would be a safe assumption."

"They'll do everything they can to attack and discredit it."

"Of course they will," he said. "Otherwise they'd have to accept it."

"But not only the message."

"No, the messenger as well."

"They'll do everything they can to attack and discredit the one who bears the message."

"Yes," said the prophet. "The messenger will be opposed, vilified and hated, mocked and slandered. It has to be that way, just as it was for Jeremiah and Baruch."

"And why was I so blessed to be chosen?" I asked.

"Why were any of us so blessed?"

With that, he approached me once more. It would be the last time.

"Had we lived in ancient times," he said, "and had we come to such a city as this, we would find it encircled by walls of stone, massive towering walls of stone for defense and security, its protection against the day of attack and calamity. All along the walls, inside its watchtowers, and above its gates stood those who kept guard...the watchmen. It was their charge to protect the city, to keep vigilant, to stay awake as the people slept, to watch, to gaze into the distance for the first sign of danger...an impending invasion. And if a watchman were to see such a sign, he would reach down to his side, pull out a ram's horn, his trumpet, set it to his mouth, and, with all his breath, sound the alarm. How do you think the watchman's alarm sounded to those inside the city?"

"Jarring, disturbing, ominous."

"Exactly.... As it had to be. If not, then those asleep would remain sleeping and those awake would never know what was coming until it was too late. Only a sound as jarring as that could save them."

He paused before continuing. "So, Nouriel, a question: Should the watchman refrain from reaching for his trumpet because the people will find it disturbing and would rather hear a pleasant sound? Or should he refuse to blow it because they'll oppose and slander him or because they'll even hate him?"

"No," I replied.

"If the watchman should see the signs of calamity appearing in the distance and fail to blow the trumpet to warn his people, what then would he become?"

"Guilty."

"Of what?"

"Of their destruction."

"Correct. He had the chance to save them but didn't. In his hand was their only hope to be saved."

"So he has no choice," I said, "but to sound it."

"And who are you, Nouriel?"

"Who *am* I?"

"Who are you?"

"I don't know."

"You're a watchman on the wall."

"A watchman on the wall..."

"A watchman on the wall who has seen the signs.... And the city sleeps...the people have no idea what's coming.... And to you is entrusted the sound of their awakening...and their redemption."

Once more the prophet was silent. And then, with the wind gusting increasingly wild and rapid, the harbinger of a coming storm, he looked intently into my eyes and began speaking the words of his final charge:

"So, then, take up your trumpet, Nouriel,

Set it to your mouth and blow,

Let the sound of the watchman be heard in the city,

Let the call of redemption cover the land,

Let the word go forth and have its way,

And let those who have ears to hear it…

Let them hear it,

And be saved."

For More Information...

To FIND OUT more on what you've read in *The Harbinger,* for related teachings or messages, for other teachings and insight from Jonathan Cahn, or for more about salvation or how to be part of God's work and End Time purposes, write to:

Hope of the World
Box 1111
Lodi, NJ 07644
USA

You can also visit his website, get in touch, and get more online at: www.TheHarbingerWebsite.com or www.HopeoftheWorld.org.

Jonathan is the leader of the Jerusalem Center/Beth Israel, a worship center made up of Jew and Gentile, people of all backgrounds, located in Wayne, New Jersey, just outside New York City.

Notes

Chapter 5—The Second Harbinger: The Terrorist

1. Isaiah 10:5–7.
2. Isaiah 10:12–16.

Chapter 6—The Oracle

1. Isaiah 9:10, translation mine. Since the original Hebrew of Isaiah 9:10 contains greater meaning than any single translation can render, throughout *The Harbinger* the words of this particular verse are translated and expounded upon directly from the original Hebrew. One standard Bible translation, the New King James Version, renders Isaiah 9:10 in this way: "The bricks have fallen down, / But we will rebuild with hewn stones; / The sycamores are cut down, / But we will replace them with cedars."

Chapter 7—The Third Harbinger: The Fallen Bricks

1. John D. W. Watts, *Word Biblical Commentary*, vol. 24 (Nashville, TN: Thomas Nelson, 1985), 143, s.v. "Isaiah 9:7–10:4."
2. D. L. Cooper, "The Book of Immanuel: Chapters 7–12," *D. L. Cooper Commentary on Isaiah*, *Biblical Research Monthly*, December 1943, http://biblicalresearch.info/page128.html (accessed June 17, 2011).

Chapter 8—The Fourth Harbinger: The Tower

1. Mayor Rudy Giuliani, September 11, 2011, quoted in "A Plan to Save the World Trade Center," TwinTowersAlliance.com, http://www.twintowersalliance.com/petition/save-the-wtc/ (accessed June 17, 2011).
2. Charles Schumer, press release, September 14, 2001.
3. Lower Manhattan Development Corporation, "Mayor Bloomberg and Governor Pataki Announce Plans to Commemorate Fifth Anniversary of the September 11th Attack," press release, August 8, 2006, http://www.renewnyc.com/displaynews.aspx?newsid=43aefabe

-5e5b-409a-98c6-0777598873b4 (accessed June 17, 2011).

4. Sweetness-Light.com, "Senator Hillary Rodham Clinton's Statement on the Floor of the United States Senate in Response to the World Trade Center and Pentagon Attacks," September 12, 2001, http://sweetness-light .com/archive/hillary-clintons-response-to-the-911-attacks (accessed June 17, 2011).

5. *New York Times*, "Mayor's Speech: 'Rebuild, Renew and Remain the Capital of the Free World,'" January 2, 2002, http://www.nytimes .com/2002/01/02/nyregion/mayoral-transition-mayor-s-speech-rebuild -renew-remain-capital-free-world.html (accessed June 17, 2011).

6. From President George W. Bush's speech to a joint session of Congress, September 20, 2001.

7. This statement is taken from the inscription on the actual sign at Ground Zero.

8. *The Interpreter's Bible*, vol. 5 (New York: Abingdon Press, 1956), 235.

9. H. D. M. Spence and Joseph S. Exell, eds., *The Pulpit Commentary*, vol. 10, Isaiah (Peabody, MA: Hendrickson Publishers, 1985), 178.

10. From the author's notes on an Expository Sermon 9, "Judgment and Grace," Isaiah 9:9–10:34, available at http://www.cliftonhillpres .pcvic.org.au/espository_sermon_9_Isaiah.

11. TheModernTribune.com, "Kerry: 'We Must Build a New World Trade Center—and Build American Resolve for a New War on Terrorism,'" speech delivered on the floor of the US Senate, September 12, 2001, as quoted in *The Modern Tribune Online*, http://www .themoderntribune.com/john_kerry_speech_after_9_11_-_rebuild_ america_and_the_world_trade_center.htm (accessed June 17, 2011).

12. Nathan Thornburgh, "The Mess at Ground Zero," *Time*, July 1, 2008, http://www.time.com/time/nation/article/0,8599,1819433,00.html (accessed June 17, 2011).

13. *The Interpreter's Bible*, 235.

14. Marcus Warren, "Ground Zero Is Reborn on the Fourth of July," *Telegraph*, July 5, 2004, http://www.telegraph.co.uk/news/worldnews/ northamerica/usa/1466250/Ground-Zero-is-reborn-on-the-Fourth-of -July.html (accessed June 17, 2011).

15. Charles F. Pfeiffer and Everett F. Harrison, eds., *The Wycliffe Bible Commentary* (Chicago: Moody Press, 1962), 620.

16. Giuliani, quoted in "A Plan to Save the World Trade Center."

17. Cooper, "The Book of Immanuel: Chapters 7–12."

18. MSNBC.com, "Trump Calls Freedom Tower 'Disgusting' and a 'Pile of Junk,'" transcript of *Hardball With Chris Matthews*, May 13, 2005, http://www.msnbc.msn.com/id/7832944/ns/msnbc_tv-hardball_with_chris_matthews/t/trump-calls-freedom-tower-disgusting-pile-junk (accessed June 17, 2011).

19. BibleStudyTools.com, "Isaiah 9," *Matthew Henry Commentary on the Whole Bible*, http://www.biblestudytools.com/commentaries/matthew-henry-complete/isaiah/9.html?p=4 (accessed June 17, 2011).

20. MSNBC.com, "Trump Calls Freedom Tower 'Disgusting' and a 'Pile of Junk.'"

21. Donald F. Ritsman, "Isaiah 9:8–10:4, Exploring the Passage," http://biblestudycourses.org/isaiah-bible-study-courses-section-1/isaiah-9-8-10-4-exploring-the-passage/ (accessed June 17, 2011).

22. Crispen Sartwell, "World Trade Center as Symbol," http://www.crispinsartwell.com/wtc2.htm (accessed June 17, 2011).

23. Sir Lancelot C. L. Brenton, *The Septuagint Version: Greek and English* (Grand Rapids, MI: Zondervan Publishing House, 1983), 844.

Chapter 9—The Fifth Harbinger: The Gazit Stone

1. StoneWorld.com, "New York Granite Is Donated for Freedom Tower," August 4, 2004, http://www.stoneworld.com/articles/new-york-granite-is-donated-for-freedom-tower (accessed June 17, 2011).

2. Port Authority of New York and New Jersey, "1,776-Foot Freedom Tower Will Be World's Tallest Building, Reclaim New York's Skyline," press release, July 4, 2004, http://www.panynj.gov/press-room/press-item.cfm?headLine_id=489 (accessed June 17, 2011).

3. Ritsman, "Isaiah 9:8–10:4, Exploring the Passage."

4. Port Authority of New York and New Jersey, "1,776-Foot Freedom Tower Will Be World's Tallest Building, Reclaim New York's Skyline."

5. Spence and Exell, eds., *The Pulpit Commentary*, vol. 10, 178.

6. Ibid.

7. "Remarks: Governor George E. Pataki, Laying of the Cornerstone for Freedom Tower, July 4, 2004," http://www.renewnyc.com/content/speeches/Gov_speech_Freedom_Tower.pdf (accessed June 21, 2011).

8. Spence and Exell, eds., *The Pulpit Commentary*, vol. 10, 178.

9. Ibid.

Chapter 11—The Seventh Harbinger: The Erez Tree

1. Spence and Exell, eds., *The Pulpit Commentary*, vol. 10, 178.
2. *The Revell Bible Dictionary* (Grand Rapids, MI: Fleming H. Revell, 1990), 198.
3. The Reverend Dr. Daniel Matthews, rector, at the dedication for the Tree of Hope at St. Paul's Chapel.
4. Ibid.
5. Matthew Henry, *Matthew Henry's Commentary on the Whole Bible,* vol. 4, *Isaiah to Malachi* (Grand Rapids, MI: Fleming H. Revell, n.d.), 61.

Chapter 12—The Eighth Harbinger: The Utterance

1. Isaiah 9:8–10.
2. Kenneth L. Barker and John Kohlenberger III, consulting editors, *The NIV Bible Commentary*, volume 1, Old Testament (Grand Rapids, MI: Zondervan Publishing House, 1994), 1,060.
3. Avalon Project at Yale Law School, "Second Inaugural Address of Abraham Lincoln, Saturday, March 4, 1865," http://avalon.law.yale.edu/19th_century/lincoln2.asp (accessed June 21, 2011).
4. John T. Woolley and Gerhard Peters, *The American Presidency Project* (online), "John Edwards: Remarks to the Congressional Black Caucus Prayer Breakfast, September 11, 2004," http://www.presidency.ucsb.edu/ws/index.php?pid=84922#axzz1M02bgo9D (accessed June 22, 2011).
5. Ibid.
6. Ibid.
7. Ibid.
8. Ibid.

Chapter 13—The Ninth Harbinger: The Prophecy

1. Library of Congress, "Bill Summary and Status, 107th Congress (2001–2002), S.J.RES.22," http://thomas.loc.gov/cgi-bin/bdquery/z?d107:s.j.res.00022: (accessed June 22, 2011).
2. Washington File, "Senate Majority Leader Daschle Expresses Sorrow, Resolve," September 12, 2001, http://wfile.ait.org.tw/wf-archive/2001/010913/epf407.htm (accessed June 22, 2011).
3. Ibid.
4. Ibid.
5. Ibid.

6. Ibid.

7. Deuteronomy 19:15.

Chapter 14—There Comes a Second

1. Spence and Exell, eds., *The Pulpit Commentary*, vol. 10, 183.

2. Gary V. Smith, *The New American Commentary* (Nashville, TN: Broadman & Holman, 2007), 247–248, s.v. "Isaiah 1:39."

3. Keil and Delitzsch, *Commentary on the Old Testament*, vol. 7, Isaiah (Grand Rapids, MI: Wm. B. Eerdmans, 1983), 258.

Chapter 15—The Isaiah 9:10 Effect

1. Isaiah 9:10, translation mine.

2. Isaiah 9:11.

3. StoneWorld.com, "New York Granite Is Donated for Freedom Tower."

4. PBS.org, "New York Stock Exchange Reopens to Sharp Losses," September 17, 2001, http://www.pbs.org/newshour/updates/september01/stock_exchange_9-17b.html (accessed June 22, 2011).

5. Gail Makinen, "The Economic Effects of 9/11: A Retrospective Assessment," Report for Congress, received through CRS Web, September 27, 2002, http://www.fas.org/irp/crs/RL31617.pdf (accessed June 22, 2011).

6. DesignFluids.com, "9/11: 'The Root' of the Financial Crisis," October 28, 2008, http://www.designfluids.com/news/911-the-root-of-the-financial-crisis-18845940 (accessed June 22, 2011).

7. CNBC.com, "House of Cards: Origins of the Financial Crisis 'Then and Now,'" slideshow, http://www.cnbc.com/id/28993790/Origins_of_the_Financial_Crisis_Then_and_Now_Slideshow (accessed June 22, 2011).

Chapter 16—The Uprooted

1. Ezekiel 13:14.

2. Jeremiah 45:4.

3. Jeremiah 45:4.

Chapter 17—The Mystery of the Shemitah

1. Leviticus 25:2–4.

2. Leviticus 25:5.

3. Exodus 23:10–11.

4. Deuteronomy 15:1–2.

5. Leviticus 26:33–35.

6. Newsweek.com, "Did Lehman's Fall Matter?," May 18, 2009, http://www.newsweek.com/2009/05/17/did-lehman-s-fall-matter.html (accessed June 23, 2011).

7. Alexandra Twin, "Stocks Crushed," CNNMoney.com, September 29, 2008, http://money.cnn.com/2008/09/29/markets/markets_newyork/index.htm (accessed June 23, 2011).

8. Ibid.

Chapter 18—The Third Witness

1. Deuteronomy 19:15.

2. 2 Corinthians 13:1.

3. WhiteHouse.gov, "Remarks of President Barack Obama—as Prepared for Delivery, Address to Joint Session of Congress, Tuesday, February 24, 2009," http://www.whitehouse.gov/the_press_office/Remarks-of-President-Barack-Obama-Address-to-Joint-Session-of-Congress/ (accessed June 23, 2011).

4. Ibid., emphasis added.

5. Ibid., emphasis added.

6. Isaiah 9:9, translation mine.

7. WhiteHouse.gov, "Remarks of President Barack Obama—as Prepared for Delivery, Address to Joint Session of Congress, Tuesday, February 24, 2009."

8. Washington File, "Senate Majority Leader Daschle Expresses Sorrow, Resolve."

9. Smith, *The New American Commentary*, 246, s.v. "Isaiah 1:39."

10. WhiteHouse.gov, "Remarks of President Barack Obama—as Prepared for Delivery, Address to Joint Session of Congress, Tuesday, February 24, 2009," emphasis added.

11. Ibid.

12. Ibid., emphasis added.

13. *Teed Commentaries*, "Isaiah Chapter 10: God's Judgment on Assyria," http://teed.biblecommenter.com/isaiah/10.htm (accessed June 23, 2011).

14. WhiteHouse.gov, "Remarks of President Barack Obama—as Prepared for Delivery, Address to Joint Session of Congress, Tuesday, February 24, 2009," emphasis added.

15. *Teed Commentaries*, "Isaiah Chapter 10: God's Judgment on Assyria."

16. WhiteHouse.gov, "Remarks of President Barack Obama—as Prepared for Delivery, Address to Joint Session of Congress, Tuesday, February 24, 2009," emphasis added.

Chapter 19—The Mystery Ground

1. Washington File, "Senate Majority Leader Daschle Expresses Sorrow, Resolve."

2. Avalon Project at Yale Law School, "First Inaugural Address of George Washington, The City of New York, Thursday, April 30, 1789," http://avalon.law.yale.edu/18th_century/wash1.asp (accessed June 23, 2011).

3. Ibid.

4. *New York Daily Advisor*, April 23, 1789, as quoted in David Barton, "The Constitutional Convention," *David Barton's Wallbuilders* (blog), July 22, 2010, http://davidbartonwallbuilders.typepad.com/blog/2010/07/the-constitutional-convention-by-david-barton.html (accessed June 23, 2011).

5. Historical Marker Database, "On This Site in Federal Hall," http://www.hmdb.org/Marker.asp?Marker=13734 (accessed June 23, 2011).

6. Avalon Project at Yale Law School, "First Inaugural Address of George Washington, The City of New York, Thursday, April 30, 1789."

Chapter 20—Things to Come

1. Henry, *Matthew Henry's Commentary on the Whole Bible*, vol. 4, *Isaiah to Malachi*, 61.

2. Isaiah 9:11.

3. Isaiah 9:12, 19; 10:3.

4. 2 Chronicles 7:14.

Chapter 22—The Last Seal

1. Jeremiah 36:4.

2. Jeremiah 36:5–6.

About the Author

אﬨ

JONATHÁN CAHN IS known for opening up the deep mysteries of Scripture and for teachings of prophetic import. He leads Hope of the World ministries, an international outreach of teaching, evangelism, and compassion projects for the needy. He also leads the Jerusalem Center/Beth Israel, a worship center made up of Jews and Gentiles, people of all backgrounds, located in Wayne, New Jersey, just outside New York City. He has ministered throughout the world and on television and radio. He is a Messianic Jewish believer, a Jewish follower of Jesus. For more information, for other messages and teaching from Jonathan, or to contact his ministry, write to:

Hope of the World
Box 1111
Lodi, NJ 07644
USA

You can also visit his website, get in touch, and get more online at: www.TheHarbingerWebsite.com or www.HopeoftheWorld.org.

If you've been touched by this book and want to see as many people as possible receive its powerful message, we invite you to join the movement of people spreading the word about...

THE HARBINGER

Many people who have read *The Harbinger* are convinced this book is a must-read for every American. Not only is this a compelling and shocking wake-up call for our nation, but its unique blend of biblical prophecy, historical events, and action-packed fictional narrative distinguishes it as a special gift. It offers one of the most unique revelations of God's love and desire to see His people return to Him that has ever been written. It will not only inspire people who already know Him with new insight into His nature but also intrigue and engage people who are not yet aware of His involvement in their lives.

The Harbinger's timely prophetic message for our country has resonated with many internationally known ministry leaders who have gotten behind the promotion of its message. As a result, within days of its release, it made the *New York Times* best-seller list and is expected to remain in high demand for a long time to come. As great as this type of promotion is, word of mouth is still the most effective way for a book to gain traction in the wider culture. If you have been moved by the message of this book, you may already be thinking of ways to let others know about it. Here are some suggestions:

- Check with your book dealer (both local and online) to see if special deals are available for bulk purchases.

- Give the book as a gift to family, friends, and even strangers. They get not only an intriguing page-turner but also insights into the nature of God that are seldom presented in our culture.

- Like the book on Facebook (www.facebook.com/theharbingerbook). Talk about the book on social media sites, websites, blogs, and other places you engage with people on the Internet. Instead of making it an advertisement, share how the book has impacted your life. Recommend that others read it as well and link them to www.theharbingerbook.com.

- Write a book review for your local paper or favorite magazine (in print or online).

- Ask your favorite radio show or podcast to have the author on as a guest.

- If you own a business, consider putting a display of these books on your counter for employees or customers.

- If you know people (authors, speakers, etc.) with a platform that enables them to speak to a wide audience, ask them to review a copy and make some comments on their websites, in newsletters, etc.

- Buy multiple copies as gifts for shelters, prisons, and rehabilitation centers where people can be provoked and encouraged by the book's timely message.

- If you're a leader, minister, speaker, communicator, or in media, let your people, your audience, or your congregation know to get it and to give it out to all who need to hear the message.

www.TheHarbingerBook.com